MYTHS, MODELS AND PARADIGMS

MYTHS, MODELS AND PARADIGMS

A Comparative Study in
Science and Religion

IAN G. BARBOUR

HARPER & ROW, PUBLISHERS

NEW YORK, HAGERSTOWN, SAN FRANCISCO, LONDON

FIRST HARPER & ROW PAPERBACK EDITION PUBLISHED IN 1976.

ISBN: 0-06-060388-7

LIBRARY OF CONGRESS CATALOG CARD NUMBER: 73-18698

85 86   10 9 8 7

CONTENTS

Contents

ACKNOWLEDGMENTS

I am indebted for comments and suggestions from a number of persons who read all or part of earlier versions of these chapters, including William H. Austin, John J. Compton, Frederick P. Ferré, Mary B. Hesse, Robert H. King, Edward A. Langerak and Perry C. Mason. Fellowships from the Guggenheim Foundation and the Fulbright exchange programme made possible a year in Cambridge, England, during which much of the research and writing was undertaken. I am grateful to the Divinity Faculty, the Philosophy of Science group, and King's College, Cambridge for their thoughtful hospitality.

I

Introduction

———

DIFFICULTIES in religious language have been described by many authors in recent years. In Germany, Rudolf Bultmann has said that modern man can no longer speak of a God who acts in nature and history and has proposed a 'demythologized' version of the gospel. In England, Bishop Robinson's *Honest to God* became a best seller, partly because of his frankness in expressing doubts about traditional ways of speaking of God. In the United States, three theologians who found themselves unable to accept theistic assertions were presented in the popular press as the 'Death of God' movement. These men are symptomatic of a widespread questioning of classical formulations.

There are many reasons for current debates about religious language. Biblical statements, if taken literally, are not credible to modern man. The God 'up there' is incompatible with our understanding of the universe. Classical discussions of the symbolic and analogical character of religious language were dependent on the metaphysical assumptions of Platonism or scholasticism, which can no longer be presupposed; more recent interpretations often hold that religious images are only symbols of man's subjective life. The possibility of meaningful language about God is widely disputed today. Theological doctrines, on the other hand, seem to be divorced from human experience. Religious ideas without an experiential basis appear abstract and irrelevant.

For other persons, the encounter of world religions has led to the adoption of a total relativism in place of exclusive claims for a particular tradition. The confidence of the Catholic community in the authority of the church and the conviction of Protestant neo-orthodoxy concerning the exclusiveness of revelation have been weakened by the new awareness of religious pluralism. The diversity of religious rituals and beliefs has been taken as support for historical and cultural relativism. Whereas teaching in theological seminaries had assumed the truth of one tradition, the growing study of religion in secular universities has been concerned about its functions in human life – without reference to the question of its truth or falsity. Often this has ended in the reductionist view that religion is entirely the product of psychological and sociological forces.

One might also point to the secularization of contemporary society, which itself has many facets: the separation of political and educational institutions from the church, the autonomy of the intellectual disciplines, the dominance of this-worldly over other-worldly interests, the confidence in man's ability to control his own destiny without divine assistance. But the present volume is concerned with the basic conceptual and methodological problems of religious language, and here the most significant influence has undoubtedly been science.

In past centuries, particular scientific theories have had a major impact on religious thought. In the eighteenth century, Newtonian mechanics led to a mechanistic view of the world and a deistic understanding of God the cosmic clockmaker. In the nineteenth century, Darwin's theory of evolution encouraged new interpretations of divine immanence in the cosmic process, as well as naturalistic philosophies of man's place in a world of law and chance. But in the twentieth century, the main influences of science on religion have come less from specific theories – such as quantum physics, relativity, astronomy, or molecular biology – than from views of science as a method.

Science seems to yield indubitable knowledge on which all men can agree. Its apparent objectivity contrasts with the subjectivity of religion. According to the popular stereotype, the scientist makes precise observations and then employs logical reasoning; if such a procedure is to be adopted in all fields of enquiry, should not religion be dismissed as prescientific superstition? And does not the scientist assume that nature is a self-contained order in which there is no place for God's action?

It has been largely through the work of philosophers that thought about the methods of science has affected religious thought in recent decades. Specifically, writings in the philosophy of science have had major repercussions in the philosophy of religion. During the 1930's and 1940's, the positivists had taken science as the norm for all meaningful discourse. Religious language was considered neither true nor false but meaningless. The positivists had proclaimed the famous Verification Principle, which states that, apart from tautologies and definitions, statements are meaningful only if they can be verified by sense data. Accepting an oversimplified view of science as the prototype for all genuine knowledge, they dismissed religion as 'purely emotive'.

During the 1950's positivism came under increasing attack, but many of its assumptions were perpetuated in the empiricism which came to replace it as the dominant interpretation of science. Among the empiricist claims were the following. (1) Science starts from publicly observable data which can be described in a pure observation-language independent of any theoretical assumptions. (2) Theories can be verified or falsified by comparison with this fixed experimental data. (3) The choice between theories is rational, objective and in accordance with specifiable criteria. Philosophers under the sway of such empiricism continued to say that religion can legitimately make no cognitive claims. We will look particularly at the protracted debate concerning the falsifiability of religious beliefs which has occurred since 1955, when Antony Flew issued his challenge to the theist: What would have to occur to constitute a disproof of the existence of God? Flew held that religious statements are not genuine assertions because the observable conditions which would falsify them cannot be specified.

But during the 1960's, the empiricist assertions listed above were vigorously criticized. It is the thesis of this volume that recent work in the philosophy of science has important implications for the philosophy of religion and for theology. Three new viewpoints concerning science, and their consequences for the critique of religion, are the central themes of the book.

The first theme, *the diverse functions of language*, reflects a change in outlook among philosophers which was already under way in the 1950's. It is well enough known that it need only be summarized here. The positivist principle that statements are meaningful only if they can be verified by sense data turned out to be too strict to satisfy even in science. The principle would have excluded scientific theories which can never be conclusively verified or proved to be immune to modification. Weaker versions were attempted, for example: a statement is meaningful only if some possible sense data are relevant to the probability of its truth or falsity. But it was extraordinarily difficult to specify at what point the 'relevance of data' was to be considered too indirect to qualify under this more generous charter.

Increasingly, philosophers came to acknowledge that language has many forms serving varied functions; science was no longer taken as the norm for all discourse. Linguistic analysis, the most prominent school of contemporary philosophy, asks how men use different types of language. Each field – science, art, ethics, religion, and so forth – has a different task, and its approach must be judged by its usefulness in accomplishing its own particular functions. The value of a statement depends on what one wants to do with it; every type of language has its own logic, appropriate to its specific purposes.

The linguistic analysts have described various functions of religious language. Sometimes it evokes and expresses self-commitment. At other times it recommends a way of life, declares an intention to act in a particular way and endorses a set of moral principles. Or again, it may propose a distinctive self-understanding and engender characteristic attitudes towards human existence. Many philosophers stress these non-cognitive functions; they insist that these tasks are valuable and legitimate but are very different from the tasks of scientific language. This is an attractive solution to issues between science and religion; the two fields cannot possibly

4

conflict if they serve totally different functions. The function of scientific language is the prediction and control of nature; that of religious language is the expression of self-commitment, ethical dedication, and existential life-orientation. But the price of this division of labour is that religion would have to give up any claims to truth, at least with respect to any facts external to one's own commitment. Religious beliefs would be useful fictions which fulfil important functions in human life but are not entitled to make any assertions. Throughout this volume a 'useful fiction' is to be regarded not as false (as in the popular usage of 'fictional'), but as neither true nor false.

The diversity of functions of religious language has also been presented in the writings of anthropologists about myths. Myths are stories which are taken to manifest some aspect of the cosmic order. They provide a community with ways of structuring experience in the present. They inform man about his self-identity and the framework of significance in which he participates. Archetypal events in primordial or historical time offer patterns for human actions today. Myths are re-enacted in rituals which integrate the community around common memories and common goals. According to many interpreters, myths are neither true nor false; they are useful fictions which fulfil these important social functions.

However, I would want to join those philosophers who also defend cognitive functions of religious language. For religion does claim to be in some sense true as well as useful. Beliefs about the nature of reality are presupposed in all the other varied uses of religious language. We can at least say that religion specifies a perspective on the world and an interpretation of history and human experience. It directs attention to particular patterns in events. It makes assertions about what is the case.

I will thus be mentioning both similarities and differences between science and religion. Existentialism and positivism, while disagreeing violently in their estimation of subjectivity, agreed completely in portraying a sharp contrast between the objectivity of science and the subjectivity of religion. I will try to show that science is not as objective, nor religion as subjective, as these two opposing schools of thought both assumed. Despite the presence of distinctive functions and attitudes in religion which have no parallels in science, there are also functions and attitudes in common, wherein I see differences of degree rather than an absolute dichotomy. Some of these comparisons are spelled out in the discussion of models and paradigms.

The second theme of the book is *the role of models*. In the last decade there has been considerable interest in model-building within many intellectual disciplines. Broadly speaking, a model is a symbolic representation of selected aspects of the behaviour of a complex system for particular purposes. It is an imaginative tool for ordering experience, rather than a description of the world. There are, of course, some objects of which actual physical replicas can be built – such as a 'scale model' of a ship or a 'working model' of a locomotive. We will be concerned, however, with mental models of systems which for various reasons cannot be represented by replicas, such as the economy of a nation, the electrons in an atom or the biblical God.

There are many types of models serving a diversity of functions. In the social sciences, models of economic development or of population growth allow quantitative predictions of a few variables to be studied under a set of simplifying assumptions. With computer models one can carry out calculations concerning the complex interaction of many variables, among which specified relationships are assumed. The simulation of the behaviour of military, industrial and urban systems is carried out in the new fields of 'operations research' and 'systems analysis'. Models of the political behaviour of an electorate are used to project election returns. Engineering models are used to solve practical problems when it is difficult to experiment on the original system.

I will deal especially with theoretical models in science, which are mental constructs devised to account for observed phenomena in the natural world. They originate in a combination of analogy to the familiar and creative imagination in the invention of the new. I will argue that theoretical models, such as the 'billard ball model' of a gas, are not merely convenient calculating devices or temporary psychological aids in the formulation of theories; they have an important continuing role in suggesting both modifications in existing theories and the discovery of new phenomena. I will try to show that such models are taken seriously but not literally. They are neither literal pictures of reality nor 'useful fictions', but partial and provisional ways of imagining what is not observable; they are symbolic representation of aspects of the world which are not directly accessible to us.

Models in religion are also analogical. They are organizing images used to order and interpret patterns of experience in human life. Like scientific models, they are neither literal pictures of reality nor useful fictions. One of the main functions of religious models is the interpretation of distinctive types of experience: awe and reverence, moral obligation, reorientation and reconciliation, interpersonal relationships, key historical events, and order and creativity in the world. I will delineate some parallels between the use of scientific models in the interpretation of observations and the use of religious models in the interpretation of experience. Ultimate models – whether of a personal God or an impersonal cosmic process – direct attention to particular patterns in events and restructure the way one sees the world.

Other functions of religious models have no parallel in science. Models in religion express and evoke distinctive attitudes. They encourage allegiance to a way of life and adherence to policies of action; their vivid imagery elicits self-commitment and ethical dedication. Religion demands existential involvement of the whole person; it asks about the ultimate objects of man's trust and loyalty. Its language expresses gratitude, dependence and worship. This self-involving and evaluational character of religion contrasts with the more detached and neutral character of science.

A separate chapter is devoted to the quesion of 'complementary models'. The term originates in modern physics, where both wave and particle models are used for electrons, photons, and other inhabitants of the atomic world. No single model is adequate for the interpretation of experiments in micro-physics, though the probability of the occurrence of particular observations can be predicted from a unified mathematical formalism. I will argue that there is some parallel in the complementarity among diverse models within religious language. I do not believe, however, that the term should be extended to call science and religion 'complementary', since they are not talking about the same phenomena and their models are of differing logical types serving differing functions.

I will suggest that the recognition that models are not pictures of reality can contribute to tolerance between religious communities. In a day when the religions of the world confront each other, the view proposed here might engender humility and tentativeness in the claims made on behalf of any one model. In place of the absolutism of exclusive claims of finality, an ecumenical spirit would acknowledge a plurality of significant religious models without lapsing into a complete relativism which would undercut all concern for truth. Analysis of models provides a path between literalism and fictionalism in religion also.

Both the cognitive claims of religion and its living practice must be grounded in experience. If inherited religious symbols are for many people today almost totally detached from human experience, a return to the experiential basis of religion is important for its renewed vitality in practice, as well as for a sound epistemology in theory. Implicit in this position, of course, is a rejection of the positivists' restriction of attention to sense-experience; all symbol-systems are selective, ordering those aspects of experience which men consider most significant.

The third theme of this volume is *the role of paradigms*. The term has received wide currency through Thomas Kuhn's influential book, *The Structure of Scientific Revolutions* (1962). Kuhn maintained that the thought and activity of a given scientific community are dominated by its paradigms, which he described as 'standard examples of scientific work that embody a set of conceptual, methodological and metaphysical assumptions'. Newton's work in mechanics, for instance, was the central paradigm of the community of physicists for two centuries. In the second edition (1970) of Kuhn's book and in subsequent essays, he distinguished several features which he had previously lumped together: a research tradition, the key historical examples ('exemplars') through which the tradition is transmitted, and the set of metaphysical assumptions implicit in its fundamental conceptual categories. Adopting these distinctions, I will use the term paradigm to refer to *a tradition transmitted through historical exemplars*. The concept of paradigm is thus defined sociologically and historically, and its implications for epistemology (the structure and character of knowledge) must be explored. Let me summarize three issues in this discussion and then indicate their implications for religion:

1. *The influence of theory on observation.* The empiricists of the 1950's had claimed that science starts from publicly observable data which can be described in a pure observation-language independent of any theoretical assumptions. By the early 1960's this claim had been challenged by a number of authors who tried to show that there is no neutral observation-language; both the procedures for making observations, and the language in which data are reported, were shown to be 'theory-laden'. Kuhn's volume gave historical illustrations of the paradigm-dependence of observations. He concluded that rival paradigms are 'incommensurable'. I will maintain that even though data are indeed theory-laden, it is possible to make pragmatic distinctions between more theoretical and more observational terms in any particular context. Rival theories are not incommensurable if their protagonists can find an overlapping core of observation-statements on which they can concur.

2. *The falsifiability of theories.* The empiricists had claimed that even though a theory cannot be verified by its agreement with data, it can be falsified by disagreement with data. But critics showed that discordant data alone have seldom been taken to falisfy an accepted theory in the absence of an alternative theory; instead, auxiliary assumptions have been modified, or the discrepancies have been set aside as anomalies. I will suggest that comprehensive theories are indeed resistant to falsification, but that observation does exert some control over theory; an accumulation of anomalies cannot be ignored indefinitely. A paradigm tradition, then, is not simply

falsified by discordant data, but is replaced by a promising alternative. Commitment to a tradition and tenacity in exploring its potentialities are scientifically fruitful; but the eventual decision to abandon it is not arbitrary or irrational.

3. *The choice between rival paradigms.* The empiricists had portrayed all scientific choices as rational, objective and in accordance with specifiable criteria. Kuhn replied that criteria for judging theories are themselves paradigm-dependent. He described the change of paradigms during a 'scientific revolution' as a matter not of logical argument but of persuasion and 'conversion'. I will argue that there are criteria of assessment independent of particular paradigms. But in the early stages, when a new contender first challenges an accepted paradigm, the criteria do not yield an unambiguous verdict; the experimental evidence and the relative weights assigned to diverse criteria are debatable and subject to individual judgment. Yet because there are accepted criteria common to all scientists, the decision can be discussed, reasons can be set forth, and an eventual consensus can be expected.

Corresponding to these three issues arising from the discussion of paradigms in science are three similar issues in religion:

1. *The influence of interpretation on experience* in religion is more problematical than the influence of theory on observation in science. There is no uninterpreted experience; but descriptions of religious experience can be given which are relatively free from doctrinal interpretation. To be sure, any set of basic beliefs tends to produce experiences which can be cited in support of those beliefs, and agreement on the data of religion seems to be exceedingly difficult to achieve. Yet because members of different religious traditions can appeal to areas of shared experience, communication is possible.

2. Flew's demand that the theist should specify *falsifying conditions* for religious beliefs seems unreasonable if such falsifying conditions cannot even be specified for comprehensive scientific theories. I will submit that though no decisive falsification is possible, the cumulative weight of evidence does count for or against religious beliefs, but with greater ambiguity than in science. Religious paradigms, like scientific ones, are not falsified by discordant data

but replaced by promising alternatives. Commitment to a paradigm (understood, again, as a tradition transmitted through historical exemplars) allows its potentialities to be systematically explored.

3. There are no *rules for choice* between religious paradigms, but there are criteria of assessment. The application of such criteria is even more subject to individual judgment in religion than in the controversies between competing paradigms during a 'scientific revolution'. Moreover religious faith includes personal trust and loyalty; it is more totally self-involving than commitment to a scientific paradigm. Nevertheless the existence of criteria means that religious traditions can be analysed and discussed. Religious commitment is not incompatible with critical reflection. It is my hope that the new views of science described here can offer some encouragement to such a combination of commitment and enquiry in religion.

These three themes – the diverse functions of language, the role of models and the role of paradigms – combine to support the position of *critical realism* which I will defend in both science and religion. Such a position recognizes the distinctive non-cognitive functions of religious language, but it also upholds its cognitive functions. Critical realism avoids naive realism, on the one hand, and instrumentalism, which abandons all concern for truth, on the other. Naive realism is untenable if models are not literal pictures of reality and if the history of science is characterized by major paradigm shifts rather than by simple cumulation or convergence. But the inadequacies of naive realism need not lead us to a fictionalist account of models, or to a total relativism concerning truth, if there are indeed data and criteria of judgment which are not totally paradigm-dependent. In the concluding chapter I will suggest some implications of critical realism for the academic study of religion and for the encounter of world religions, as well as for personal religious faith.

2

Symbol and Myth

———

IN THIS CHAPTER I wish briefly to consider religious models in relation to other forms of religious language – particularly symbols, images and myths. Four issues which will be significant in the subsequent analysis of models arise here in discussing these other linguistic forms: (1) the role of analogy, (2) the relation of religious symbolism to human experience, (3) the diverse functions of religious language (especially evident in the case of myth) and (4) the cognitive status of religious language. I will suggest that the idea of religious models offers a distinctive way of dealing with each of these issues.

1. METAPHOR AND SYMBOL

Because religious language is frequently metaphorical, I start with some remarks about metaphors in general. A metaphor proposes *analogies* between the normal context of a word and a new context into which it is introduced. Some, but not all, of the familiar connotations of the word are transferred. 'The lion is king of the beasts', but it has only some of the attributes of royalty. 'Love is a fire', but we do not expect it to cook a meal. There is a tension between affirmation and negation, for in analogy there are both similarities and differences.

The philosopher Max Black argues that in *metaphoric usage* there is a highly selective transfer of some of the familiar associations of a word. These associations then act as a kind of screen or lens through which the new subject is viewed; some of its features are ignored or suppressed while others are emphasized or distinctively organized. It is seen in a new way and new attitudes are evoked. Thus the expression 'Man is a wolf' invites us to consider human traits which might be analogous to familiar wolf-traits. We are to construe man as wolf-like, or, in general, to 'construe one situation in terms of another'. A metaphor can order our perceptions, bringing forward aspects which we had not noticed before. One kind of experience is interpreted in terms of the characteristics of another.[1]

In a metaphor, a novel configuration has been produced by the juxtaposition of *two frames of reference* of which the reader must be simultaneously aware. I. A. Richards calls it a 'transaction between contexts'. It is a new creation for which there are no rules, and 'its meaning survives only at the intersection of the two perspectives which produced it'.[2] One must maintain an awareness of both contexts illuminating each other in unexpected ways. There is often novelty and surprise in these new combinations and the fresh images that they evoke. They arise from the concreteness and individuality of particular experiences, which only an extension of language can try to convey.

A metaphor is *not literally true*. Imagine someone getting out the scales when his friend says 'My heart is heavy', or asking for salt and pepper upon hearing 'She has been in a stew all day'. A metaphor is absurd if interpreted literally because the two contexts are widely disparate; there is a flagrant crossing of what philosophers call 'type-boundaries'. Yet a metaphor is not a useful fiction, a mere pretence, a game of make-believe with no relation to reality; it asserts that there are significant analogies between the things compared.

Literary critics have debated at length whether these resemblances can be reduced to a set of *equivalent literal expressions*. Some critics have said that a metaphor is a condensed simile or a substitute for detailed comparison; they claim that a metaphor can be paraphrased exactly by a set of statements about the resemblance of specific features of the two situations. The metaphor's function would then be decorative and rhetorical, contributing vividness and style but no distinctive cognitive content. It would have a psychological role but not an indispensable logical one.

The opposing view, with which I would side, holds that a metaphor cannot be replaced by a set of equivalent literal statements because it is *open-ended*. No limits can be set as to how far the comparison might be extended; it cannot be paraphrased because it has an unspecifiable number of potentialities for articulation.[3] The comparison is left for the reader to explore. It is not an illustration of an idea already explicitly spelled out, but a suggestive invitation to the discovery of further similarities. It will be proposed in the next chapter that scientific models are not eliminable because they, too, are based on analogies which are open-ended and extensible, though of course they are more systematically developed than metaphors.

Unlike scientific models, however, metaphors – especially in poetry – often have *emotional and valuational overtones*. They call forth feelings and attitudes. Metaphors are dynamic; language becomes event. The reader is involved as a personal participant and is encouraged to draw from various dimensions of his own experience. Metaphor is expressive of the poet's experience and evocative of the reader's. But the presence of these non-cognitive functions does not require that cognitive functions be absent. Metaphors influence *perception and interpretation* as well as attitude. A poem, according to Philip Wheelwright, 'says something, however tentatively and obliquely, about the nature of what is'. Even though it makes only 'a shy ontological claim', it is not just emotional. It makes a 'light assertion' which is referential even when it is only suggestive. It is judged by its faithfulness to concrete human experience.[4]

Now many religious symbols seem to be metaphors based on analogies within man's experience. Consider first the *symbols of height*. Movement upwards is physically more difficult than downwards, so 'higher' becomes a symbol of achievement and excellence (think of the imagery of 'ascent', from Plato to Dante to Thomas Merton). Height is also associated with the recognition of power, as when men kneel or bow down before the elevated throne of a king in acknowledging his rule 'over' them. Edwyn Bevan shows, more specifically, that the sense of religious awe is similar to the awe in looking up at a mountain or at the sky. Symbols of height are therefore appropriate expressions of worship, e.g. 'the high and lofty One'.[5]

The frequency of *symbolism of light* in religion seems to rest on several analogies. A person can see better in the light which therefore becomes a symbol of knowledge; this is evident in the cognate verbs for imparting knowledge ('illuminate', 'clarify', 'illustrate', 'throw light on') or the adjective 'bright'. Light symbolism is frequent in Platonism and gnosticism, in Buddhist 'enlightenment', in such deities as Mazda in Iran or Agni in Vedic India, in biblical assertions that 'God is light', and so forth. Perhaps also there are analogies between the experience of standing in a dazzling or blinding light and moments of religious exaltation, reflected in the Hebrew idea of God's 'glory' or Paul's phrase, 'light unapproachable'.[6]

A symbol may have quite diverse meanings corresponding to the diversity of contexts in which the analogue was originally encountered. *Water* is a symbol of chaos (the primeval waters, for instance) but also of regeneration and purification (as in baptism), since man experiences water both as a destructive power and as a cleansing agent and sustainer of life. Similarly *fire* can at various times be devouring, purifying or life-giving. Furthermore, a number of differing metaphors may be applied to the same religious experience. Thus the Christian experience of liberation from anxiety and guilt is variously described as analogous to acquittal in a law court, the release of a slave, the ransom of a captive, the reconciliation of enemies, the forgiveness of one person by another and the recovery of health after sickness.[7]

Whereas poetic metaphors are used only momentarily, in one context, for the sake of an immediate impression or insight, *religious symbols* become part of the language of a religious community in its scripture and liturgy and in its continuing life and thought. Religious symbols are expressive of man's emotions and feelings, and are powerful in calling forth his response and commitment. They arise from personal participation, not detached observation; they are rooted in man's experience as an active subject. But they need not

15

be taken literally; they combine affirmation and negation and point beyond themselves. As Tillich puts it, a religious symbol is idolatrous unless it suggests its own inadequacy.[8]

In the biblical tradition, many of the dominant metaphors are drawn from personal agency, with its categories of intention, purpose, will, action and promise. Some personal analogues are referred to infrequently, for example, 'The Lord is my Shepherd'. Others are invoked more often and developed more systematically, becoming what I shall call *models*, for instance, 'God is a Father to his children'. Metaphors are employed only momentarily and symbols only in a limited range of contexts, but models are more fully elaborated and serve as wider interpretive schemes in many contexts. We are asked, in the biblical case, to construe the world through the model of a father's love and purpose. Other religious traditions have used dominant models which are impersonal in character.

In later chapters we will find that religious models, like literary metaphors, influence *attitudes and behaviour* and also alter *ways of seeing the world*. They serve as 'organizing images' which give emphasis, selectively restructuring as well as interpreting our perceptions. Models, like metaphors, may help us to notice particular features of the world. In all of these functions – the evocation of attitudes, the guidance of behaviour, the interpretation of experience, and the organization of perceptions – a metaphor is used only momentarily, whereas a model is used in a sustained and systematic fashion. In both cases, however, claims are made about the world and not simply about human feelings and attitudes.

2. PARABLE AND ANALOGY

A narrative form of analogy frequently found in religious teachings is the *parable*, a short fictional story whose characters are taken from everyday life. In an allegory, every person or part represents something else with a 1-to-1 correspondence; in a parable, however, the story as a whole conveys the comparison (for example, 'The Kingdom of God is like unto a man who . . .'). I will confine myself to three observations:

1. *Parables call for decision.* They suggest attitudes and policies and provoke the hearer's response. His judgment is called for; he must accept or reject. Occasionally this is explicitly pointed out; King David acknowledges that the poor man in Nathan's parable has been unjustly treated and then sees that this implies a condemnation of himself. More often the hearer is implicitly invited to see himself in a parable; he is drawn in as participant and actor. Peter Slater has written:

> The analogies developed in parables are not just any analogies. They are those which help us to develop our policies for living and decide on their adoption. The central analogies are ones which suggest roles and rules in life, such as the role of sonship and the rule of neighbourly love. They are rarely analogies to impersonal features of the universe, designed to aid in speculating about anything as abstruse as 'being as such'.[9]

Some parables, such as the Parable of the Good Samaritan, are indeed 'useful fictions' whose only point is to recommend attitudes, policies for living, 'rules and roles'. Other parables seem at the same time to make claims about reality; the Parable of the Prodigal Son commends to us a filial stance, but it also implies that God is like a father.

2. *Parables are open-ended.* C. H. Dodd gives this definition: 'At its simplest, the parable is a metaphor or simile, drawn from nature or common life, arresting the hearer by its vividness or strangeness, and leaving the mind in sufficient doubt about its precise application to tease it into active thought.'[10] Like a metaphor, a parable presents a comparison to be explored, insights to be discovered, not an optional illustration of a set of explicitly stated principles. (Most scholars believe that the explanations, allegories and hortatory appeals which follow several of Jesus' parables in the gospels were later additions to the parables themselves.[11]) Often parables are many-faceted and can be applied to one's own situation under a variety of circumstances after one has tried to understand the original context in which they were told.

3. *Parables communicate vivid images.* Who can forget the Prodigal Son, or the Good Samaritan, once he has heard about them? Mental images are more important than abstract concepts as vehicles for

the transmission of a religious tradition. Images influence attitudes and behaviour more powerfully than general principles do. They are common in the experience of worship (as, for example, in the temple imagery of Isaiah's vision). Perhaps both philosophers and theologians, in concentrating on verbally-stated propositions, have tended to neglect the role of images in human thought.[12]

Austin Farrer maintains that *religious images* are central in the biblical tradition. He holds that God has revealed himself through 'inspired images' rather than through creeds or doctrines. These images, he urges, are based on analogies which man neither postulates nor establishes for himself, but simply accepts because they are 'God-given'. Once revealed, they can be used to interpret experience and historical events. Farrer discusses a number of these biblical images in detail and makes a convincing case for their influence.[13]

The idea of '*directly revealed images*' escapes the literalism of directly revealed propositions, yet several objections can be raised. By his appeal to authority, Farrer makes 'authorized images' immune to criticism. Surely the images of different religious traditions lead to incompatible affirmations. On what basis should one accept the claim that the images of a particular tradition are revealed? Further, can we not acknowledge the importance of imagination without treating it as a separate faculty which God could use in isolation from other faculties? To be sure, Farrer does give the religious community an active role in the development and interpretation of images, and even in their origination man is not entirely passive. But by detaching religious images from the human experience in which they occur, he minimizes the influence of psychological forces and cultural images (from literature, mythology, art, etc.). I would agree that in the biblical tradition events are interpreted through dominant images, but I submit that the images themselves are not directly God-given but arise from man's analogical imagination.

The role of analogy which I will develop differs, however, from *the traditional doctrine of analogy*. How can religious language avoid literalism on the one hand and emptiness on the other? If familiar terms are predicated of God literally (univocally), one ends in anthropomorphism. But if no familiar terms can be predicated, except equivocally, one ends in agnosticism. (If divine love in no way resembles human love, the term is vacuous; one could as well call it divine hate, or divine obesity, after disclaiming all familiar denotations of the terms.) The doctrine of analogy was supposed to provide a middle way, allowing for both similarity and difference between God and man.[14]

But one of its two classical forms, the *analogy of proportionality*, seems to end close to agnosticism. For it denies that there is any analogy between divine and human goodness themselves; it asserts only that divine goodness is to God's nature as human goodness is to man's nature – in other words, that each is good in a way appropriate to its own nature. But unless we have some prior knowledge of God's nature, or assume an ontology of 'levels of being' with some continuity between the levels, the 'proportionality' tells us nothing about God. The other classical form, the *analogy of attribution*, states that a characteristic can be predicated 'formally' of God and 'derivatively' of created things. But the argument rests on the assumptions that causes resemble their effects and that God is the cause of the world. The conclusion then asserts only what was already in the premiss: the creator is good in whatever way necessary to produce goodness in the creatures. If analogies are based on religious experience, however, neither of these two assumptions need be made. The role of analogy in religious models will be presented in a later chapter.

3. THE CHARACTER OF MYTH

Religious symbols and images are combined in the complex narratives known as myths. These forms have been illuminated by historians studying ancient civilizations and by anthropologists studying preliterate cultures today. In contrast to literary critics, who have usually concentrated on the internal content of myths, historians and anthropologists have been concerned about their place in the lives of individuals and groups. In broad terms, a myth is *a story which is taken to manifest some aspect of the cosmic order*. We shall for the moment postpone the question of the relation of the events narrated in the myth to historical events, and consider the function of myths in human life. Unlike a fairy tale, a living myth is highly significant in personal and corporate life; it endorses particular ways of ordering experience and acting in daily life, along the following lines:

1. *Myths offer ways of ordering experience.* Myths provide a world-view, a vision of the basic structure of reality. Most myths are set at the time of creation, or in a primordial time, or at the time of key historical events – times in which the forms of existence were established, modified or disclosed. The present is interpreted in the light of the formative events narrated in the myth, as Mircea Eliade has shown. Peter Berger refers to this ordering of experience as 'nomizing' or 'cosmizing', the adoption of a dramatized cosmic framework for human life. According to Streng, myths show 'the essential structure of reality, manifest in particular events of the past that are remembered from generation to generation'. A myth is relevant to daily life because it deals with perennial problems and the enduring order of the world in which man lives.[15]

2. *Myths inform man about himself.* He takes his self-identity in part from the past events which he believes have made him what he is. He understands himself in relation to the ancestors of his people. A community is constituted by the key events which it remembers and in which its members participate. A living myth evokes personal involvement rather than contemplation or conceptual analysis. It is a way of action which brings man into accord with a group and an ordained order. It expresses 'the continuity between the structures of human existence and cosmic structures' (Eliade). Creation myths usually manifest in dramatic form basic convictions about human nature and destiny.

3. *Myths express a saving power in human life.* The cosmic order reflected in myths typically has a tri-partite structure. There is an *ideal* state or being which represents the source, ground and goal of life. The *actual* condition of man is separated from the ideal by some flaw, defect or distortion, variously understood as sin, ignorance,

attachment, etc. But a *saving power* can overcome the flaw and establish the ideal; it may take the form of a personal redeemer, or a law, ritual or discipline to be followed. Myths thus portray and convey a power to transform man's life, rather than a predominantly theoretical explanation of it.

4. *Myths provide patterns for human actions.* They hold up not an abstract ideal but a prototype for man's imitation. Often the actions of divine beings or mythical ancestors give the exemplary patterns for ritual, moral and practical behaviour. 'Hence the supreme function of the myth is to "fix" the paradigmatic models for all rites and all significant activities – eating, sexuality, work, education, etc.'[16] Myths are vivid and impressive, inspiring their adherents to emotional response and concrete action. They encourage particular forms of behaviour and implicitly embody ideal goals and judgments of value. Myths form and sanction the moral norms of a society.

5. *Myths are enacted in rituals.* Myths are expressed, not only in symbolic words, but also in symbolic acts – dance, gesture, drama, and formalized cultic acts or rites. Myths are narrated and enacted in rituals. The myth often justifies the ritual, while the ritual transmits the myth and provides a way of taking part in it, as van der Leeuw shows.[17] The original event becomes present (re-presented) in symbolic re-enactment. Cultic acts embody the creative power of primordial and historical time and create anew the forms for ordering experience and action.

There are many examples of this close association of myth and ritual. New Year's festivals in several cultures are known to have included the *recitation and enactment* of creation myths. In ancient Mesopotamia, the victory of Marduk over Tiamat, the primeval dragon, was acted out annually; the New Year, as a new beginning, was celebrated as a renewal of the primordial victory of order over chaos. There was a close correlation of myth and ritual also in the 'mystery religions' of the Near East, such as Orphic, Eleusinian and Isis cults. The latter was a ritual dramatization of the Isis–Osiris myth of death and resurrection, through which the initiate sought immortality. Again, the 'rites of passage' at critical points in individual life, marking a change of status (birth, puberty, marriage, death), are almost always accompanied by the presentation of myths. Initiation ceremonies and rites of purification and rebirth are rich in mythical symbolism.[18]

Some anthropologists have in fact maintained that *ritual was the earliest form* in all religious traditions, and that myth was developed later to justify and explain ritual. Marett holds that 'men danced out before they thought out their responses'. Changes in behaviour and in action often occur before changes in ideas. Thus Hyman, Raglan, and others[19] claim that myth arises from rite – even though the myth may be remembered long after the rite which it sanctioned has disappeared. Other anthropologists, such as Clyde Klukhohn,[20] reply that there are some myths (among African Pygmy and American Indian tribes, for example,) which have evidently never been enacted in ceremonial form. They insist that the interaction between myth and ritual is complex and diverse, and cannot be reduced to any simple universal pattern except by a selective use of evidence. In some cases myth influences ritual, in other cases ritual influences myth, in still others they develop together – or separately – according to particular needs and historical circumstances.

Both myth and ritual are frequently *forms of celebration*. Agricultural communities have celebrated the life-giving and creative forces in the world, rejoicing in the wonder of renewed life in the spring, and joining in festivals of thanksgiving for harvest in the autumn. The festivals and holy days of ancient Israel were primarily celebrations of the historical events which it remembered and symbolically re-enacted. The liturgy, ritual and sacraments of the Christian community have, of course, centered on its memory of the life of Christ. In all these instances, man's life in the present is interpreted in relation to the cosmic order portrayed in stories about the past.

If a myth is defined as a story in which some aspect of the cosmic order is manifest, then the *scriptures* of Judaism, Christianity and Islam must be said to include myths. For in them one finds stories of God's creation, judgment, deliverance, incarnation, and so forth; and these stories offer ways of ordering experience and patterns for human action and ritual re-enactment. In the western religions, myth is indeed tied primarily to historical events rather than to phenomena in nature. This difference is crucial for conceptions of history, time and ethics, but it need not lead us to deny the presence of myth in the Bible. Divine action is in itself no more directly observable in history than in primordial time or in nature.[21]

The broad definition given would include *modern secular philosophies* whose stories, while not about the gods, do deal with 'aspects of the cosmic order'. Marxism and evolutionary naturalism are world-visions with most of the characteristics described above. Some authors speak of modern 'covert myths' of inevitable progress, human rationality, and utopia through technology.[22] We will be mainly concerned, however, with traditional religious myths.

4. THE FUNCTIONS OF MYTH

We must now examine the functions and cognitive status of myths and relate them to models. Consider first *the psychological functions* of myths for the individual. In the face of the insecurities of illness, natural disaster and death, myths and rituals contribute to the reduction of anxiety.[23] They are a mechanism of ego defense against a variety of threats to human welfare, and a way of restoring the individual's rapport with nature and society. They are a source of security and a symbolic resolution of conflicts. In the psychoanalytic interpretation, myths, like individual dreams, are symbolic expressions of unconscious wishes. According to Freud, they are collective fantasies representing repressed sexual impulses. Freudian authors find disguised sexual symbolism and forgotten childhood experiences (e.g., incestual desires or hatred of father or mother) behind every myth.[24]

The *social functions* of myth have been stressed by other interpreters since Durkheim. Myths promote the integration of society. They are a cohesive force binding a community together and contributing to social solidarity, group identity and communal harmony. They encourage cultural stability, for 'myth is an active force which is intimately related to almost every aspect of culture'

(Malinowski). Myth sanctions the existing social order and justifies its status system and power structure, providing a rationale for social and political institutions – from kinship to kingship. A common morality is supported by a mythical tradition, which perpetuates both value-attitudes and specific behavioural recommendations.

An interesting interpretation known as *structuralism* has been expounded by Claude Lévi-Strauss. He finds a binary structure in many myths with opposing terms. These myths have an internal logical pattern in which the initial opposition is overcome, often by the introduction of a third term. But the formal properties of the myth, especially the logic of contradictions and correlations, have parallels in the structure of society. The binary oppositions in society are made tolerable by the myth; the third category helps to mediate between the overtly irreconcilable aspects of the social order. Thus Lévi-Strauss tries to display the linguistic and logical features of the recurrent patterns within various myths, and to set forth their function in coping with conflicts in individual and social life.[25]

Now these analyses of various psychological and social functions do not in themselves say anything about *the cognitive status* of myth. To be sure, if any one of these analyses is taken as an all-embracing theory concerning the origins of myth, it becomes a reductionist explanation. (This occurs if one says that myth is nothing but a projection of sexual repression, or nothing but a rationalization of ritual or a symbolic representation of social structures.) But it would be quite consistent to defend a variety of functions of myth in individual and social life, while leaving to one side the question of truth or falsity. To the instrumentalist, however, a myth is in principle neither true nor false, but *a useful fiction*. Thus Alasdair MacIntyre writes:

> A myth is living or dead, not true or false. You cannot refute a myth because as soon as you treat it as refutable, you do not treat it as a myth but as a hypothesis or history. Myths which could not easily coexist if they were hypotheses or histories, as for example rival accounts of creation, can comfortably belong to the same body of mythology.[26]

But surely the problem of the cognitive status of myths cannot be so easily dismissed. For one thing, *the belief systems* of religious traditions are taken more seriously by their adherents than instrumentalist accounts acknowledge. Cosmological beliefs are a central feature of myth, as Eliade has indicated. De Waal Malefijt maintains that myth and ritual are intimately associated, not because either is derived from the other, but because both are based on particular beliefs about the cosmic order.[27] A ritual presupposes a world-view, a set of assumptions within which the ritual makes sense. Henry Murray describes 'cognitive and convictional functions' of myths, which must be credible to their adherents, though he considers these secondary to other functions.[28] Even though a living myth is closer to daily life than to metaphysical speculation, it does seem to presuppose some sort of truth-claims which can be examined.

What cognitive status, then, can be assigned to myth? In the nineteenth century, mythology was usually viewed as a *primitive attempt to explain natural phenomena*. One could point to etiological stories accounting for the origins of striking features of the world and then conclude that myths are essentially prescientific attempts to answer scientific questions. As such, they have obviously been superseded by modern science. Influenced by the prevailing faith in man's progress and the evolution of culture, these authors dismissed myth as the product of the prelogical mind during 'the childhood of the race'. Even Ernst Cassirer – who defends myth as an autonomous form irreducible to psychological or social forces, and holds that myths are based on an authentic intuition of the solidarity and continuity of cosmic life – ends by asserting that the age of mythical consciousness has been superseded by the scientific age.[29]

But if myths are not true when taken literally, what kind of truth can they be said to have? One possibility would be to take them as *symbols of man's inner life*. They would be valid in so far as they authentically expressed man's feelings, hopes and fears, or his experiences of guilt, reconciliation and liberation from anxiety. Carl Jung goes further than this: for him, myths are the projection of inner psychic dramas, but these in turn are products of the 'collective unconscious'. Common to the mythologies of the ancient world and the dreams of modern man, he says, are archetypal figures, primordial images, universal symbols, known by a kind of immediate intuitive awareness. Even myths about the elements of nature (sun and moon, summer and winter, etc.) are symbolic expressions of man's unconscious psychic life in which the eternal archetypes are encountered.[30]

The most notable recent effort to translate biblical myth in terms of man's inner life is Rudolf Bultmann's programme of '*demythologizing*'. He objects to myth because it tries to represent the divine in the objective categories of the physical world. In the New Testament these misleading categories include space (e.g., Christ as 'coming down' and 'ascending'), time (eschatology as temporal finality), and causality (miracles and supernatural forces). These first-century thought-forms must be rejected, according to Bultmann, both because they are scientifically untenable in a world of lawful cause-and-effect and because they are theologically inadequate: the transcendent cannot be represented in the categories of the objective world. Moreover, he insists, the true meaning of scriptural myth always did involve man's self-understanding. The gospel was concerned about man's hopes, fears, decisions and commitments in the present, not about miraculous occurrences in the past.[31]

For Bultmann, 'demythologizing' is accomplished by *existential re-interpretation*. All religious formulations must be statements of a new understanding of ourselves. We must ask what a given myth says about new modes of personal existence, new possibilities for our lives. Bultmann draws from the categories of Heidegger's philosophy: man's anxiety, fallenness and guilt, and the transition to authenticity, freedom and openness to the future. Christ was the man of radical freedom – freedom from anxiety, freedom to love – and he opens for us the possibility of authentic existence. Faith is not the acceptance of propositions about the past but response, decision and reorientation in the present. Here is a comprehensive programme for translating mythical imagery into the language of personal experience.

But the price of this *internalization of myth* is a neglect of God's relation to nature and history. I would grant that God is not encountered apart from personal involvement, without granting that God's action is limited to the sphere of selfhood. Bultmann maintains the existentialist dichotomy between the sphere of personal selfhood and the sphere of impersonal objects, perpetuating the Kantian bifurcation of man and nature. In this retreat to interiority, nature becomes the impersonal stage for the drama of personal existence. One wonders also whether the gospel has not been dehistoricized. The message concerning Christ can indeed be an occasion of personal reorientation, but what is the significance of the event itself? Did God act in history, or does he act only in the present transformation of man's life? In short, has Bultmann by subjectivizing myth lost its reference to nature and history?

The alternative which I am proposing is to consider the *models* which are embodied in myths. Models, like metaphors, symbols and parables, are analogical and open-ended. Metaphors, however, are used only momentarily, and symbols and parables have only a limited scope, whereas models are systematically developed and pervade a religious tradition. A model represents the enduring structural components which myths dramatize in narrative form. One model may be common to many myths. A model is relatively static and lacks the imaginative richness and dramatic power which make a myth memorable; men will always express their understanding of the meaning of life by telling stories and enacting them in rituals. Models result from reflection on the living myths which communities transmit. In the remainder of this volume we must keep in mind this wider context: the life of religious communities.

Models summarize the structural elements of a set of myths. They can represent aspects of the cosmic order, including nature and history, which are dramatized in myth but which tend to be neglected in Bultmann's de-mythologized existentialism. Like myths, models offer ways of ordering experience and of interpreting the world. They are neither literal pictures of reality nor useful fictions. They lead to conceptually formulated, systematic, coherent, religious beliefs which can be critically analyzed and evaluated. These *cognitive* functions of religious models in *the interpretation of experience* present a number of parallels with the functions of theoretical models in science which will be explored in subsequent chapters.

But religious models can also fulfil many of the *non-cognitive* functions of myth, particularly in *the expression of attitudes*; these functions have no parallel in science. Models embodied in myths evoke commitment to ethical norms and policies of action. Like metaphors, religious models elicit emotional and valuational responses. Like parables, they encourage decision and personal involvement. Like myths, they offer ways of life and patterns of behaviour. Analysis of models thus provides an illuminating method of dealing with the cognitive functions of myths without neglecting non-cognitive functions. We will return to these diverse characteristics of religious models in Chapter 4 below.

3

Models in Science

THERE ARE IN science a number of different kinds of model which serve a diversity of functions.[1] They are used, that is, for very diverse purposes. First there are *experimental models* which can actually be constructed and used in the laboratory. These include replicas or 'scale models' representing spatial relationships, and 'working models' representing temporal sequences. From a wind-tunnel model of a proposed airplane design, the lifting force of a particular wing structure can be estimated. In an 'analogue model', certain features of one system are simulated by the behaviour of another system in a different medium – for instance, a hydraulic flow model of an economic system, or an electrical circuit model of an acoustic system. Such models are used to solve practical problems when it is difficult to experiment on the primary system, or when the relevant mathematical equations are unknown or too complex to solve. In these cases one physical system is actually built to serve as a model of another physical system.[2]

Second, at the opposite extreme, there are *logical models*. The logician or the pure mathematician starts from the axioms and theorems of a formal deductive system. A logical model is a particular set of entities which satisfy these axioms and theorems. For example, a set of points and lines in geometry is a logical model for Euclid's formal axioms. The mathematician uses it to illustrate the abstract system and to give a possible interpretation of it. Note that here he is dealing entirely in the realm of ideas; neither the formal system nor the model of it are physical systems.[3]

Third, *mathematical models* are between these two extremes. They are symbolic representations of quantitative variables in physical or social systems. Examples might be: equations proposed to express the relation between supply and demand in economics, or the growth of a population in time. A mathematical model may in turn be physically represented by the electrical circuits of a computer; computer models of economic, political, military and transportation systems are widely used today. At the moment, the point to note is that a mathematical model resembles the primary system only in formal structure; there are no material or physical similarities. It is a symbolic representation of particular aspects of a physical system, and its chief use is to predict the behaviour of the latter.

My main concern in this chapter is a fourth kind, *theoretical models*. These are imaginative mental constructs invented to account for observed phenomena. Such a model is usually an imagined mechanism or process, which is postulated by analogy with familiar mechanisms or processes. I will maintain that its chief use is to help one understand the world, not simply to make predictions. But I will also claim that it is not a literal picture of the world. Like a mathematical model, it is a symbolic representation of a physical system, but it differs in its intent to represent the underlying structure of the world. It is used to develop a theory which in some sense explains the phenomena. And its origination seems to require a special kind of creative imagination. In the subsequent chapter theoretical models will be compared with models in religion.

I. THEORETICAL MODELS

A theoretical model, then, is an imagined mechanism or process, postulated by *analogy* with familiar mechanisms or processes and used to construct a *theory* to correlate a set of *observations*. I will call the source of the analogy 'the familiar system', where 'familiar' means better understood rather than everyday. The model drawn from the familiar system suggests a theory. It also suggests possible relationships between some of the terms of the theory and some observation terms; these correlations linking theory and observation are called 'rules of correspondence'. A theoretical model, in short, is used to generate a theory to explain the behaviour of an observable system. The relation of theory and observation is examined in Chapter 6 below. In the present chapter attention is directed to the distinctive role of models in the generation of theories.

Let me give an illustration from physics since it is the scientific field I know best: the *'billiard-ball model'* of a gas. Consider a box full of a gas, such as air, and imagine that the gas is composed of very tiny elastic spheres bouncing around. If one assumes that the mechanical behaviour of the hypothetical spheres is similar to the familiar behaviour of colliding billiard balls, a theory can be developed (the Kinetic Theory of Gases). The theory involves equations interrelating the mass (m), velocity (v), energy and momentum of the hypothetical spheres. Of course none of these theoretical properties can be observed. But the model also intimates that some theoretical terms might be related to observable properties of the gas (for example, the momentum change of the 'particles' colliding with the containing wall might be identified with the pressure of the gas). With these assumptions one can derive several of the well-known experimental Gas Laws – Boyle's Law, for instance, which states that if the volume (V) of a gas is reduced by 50% (by compressing the air in a bicycle pump, for example) then the pressure (P) of the gas will double.

The *model* thus leads to a *theory*, and the theory accounts for patterns in experimental *observations*. These ralationships are portrayed schematically in the diagram.

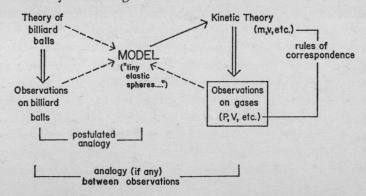

The double arrows signify the formal deduction of experimental laws from the theory together with rules of correspondence. Three features of the billiard-ball model, and others like it, should be noted:

1. *Models are analogical.* Similarities with a familiar situation are posited in some respects (the positive analogy), and differences are posited in other respects (the negative analogy). Thus our hypothetical tiny elastic spheres were assumed to have mass and velocity, as billiard balls do, but not colour. Notice that the analogies postulated may be physical (e.g., elasticity and mass), and not simply formal as in the case of logical or mathematical models. In the origination of a novel theory the scientist may propose a model incorporating analogies drawn from several familiar situations, together with radically new assumptions. In the diagram all the lines going *into* the model are shown dotted because its origins lie in an act of creative imagination and not in purely logical inference. In general, we would have to show additional dotted arrows coming in from other familiar situations at the left. In imagining a model there is implicit or explicit reference to what is familiar and previously intelligible, but there is also considerable novelty and freedom. One can assign to it whatever properties one thinks might contribute fruitfully to the theory.

The history of science provides many examples of this combination of *analogy* and *innovation* in the creation of models which were useful in generating theories.[4] The 'Bohr model' of the atom, in which 'planetary' electrons revolve in orbits around a central nucleus, resembles the solar system in certain of its dynamical properties; but the key assumption of quantum jumps between orbits had no classical parallel at all. Again, the model of vibrating oscillators was prominent in the development of a theory of the specific heat of metals. Among more recent examples is the 'liquid drop model' of the nucleus. Somewhat different in character, but equally crucial in the origination and interpretation of a theory, is the model of an ideal heat engine in the field of thermodynamics. In each case the model aided the formulation of the equations of the theory and also suggested rules of correspondence between certain theoretical terms and observable variables.

2. *Models contribute to the extension of theories.* The use of a model may encourage the postulation of new rules of correspondence and the application of a theory to new kinds of phenomena. Thus the equations of the Kinetic Theory were applied to new experimental domains (including gas diffusion, viscosity and heat conduction) which involved types of observation very different from those of the gas laws. A model may also be crucial in the modification of the theory itself. It was the model, not the formalism of the theory, which led to the hypothesis of particles having a finite size and attracting each other; when the theory was thus amended, van der Waal's equations for gases under high pressure could be derived. The revised model (elastic spheres with attractive forces) departs from the simple billiard-ball model, yet it would never have occurred to anyone without the latter. As Mary Hesse points out, clues for the modification of a theory often arise in exploring the 'neutral analogy' – that is, the features of the familiar situation whose inclusion in the model has neither been explicitly affirmed nor denied.[5] She argues that because of its suggestiveness and open-endedness, a model is a continuing source of plausible hypotheses:

> The theoretical model carries with it what has been called 'open texture' or 'surplus meaning', derived from the familiar system. The theoretical model conveys associations and implications that are not completely specifiable and that may be transferred by analogy to the explanandum [the phenomenon to be explained]; further developments and modifications of the explanatory theory may therefore be suggested by the theoretical model. Because the theoretical model is richer than the explanandum, it imports concepts and conceptual relations not present in the empirical data alone.[6]

3. *A model is intelligible as a unit.* It provides a mental picture whose unity can be more readily understood than that of a set of abstract equations. A model is grasped as a whole; it gives in vivid form a summary of complex relationships. It is said to offer 'epistemological immediacy' or 'direct presentation of meaning'. Because of its vividness and intelligibility it is frequently used for teaching purposes to help a student understand a theory. But even at the critical stages of scientific discovery itself, scientists report that visual imagery often predominates over verbal or mathematical

thinking, according to several studies.[7] Images are creative expressions of the human imagination in the sciences as in the humanities. There are of course, no rules for creativity; but it has been pointed out that analogies, models and metaphors are common in the search for new kinds of connection and new ways of looking at phenomena.[8] Campbell suggests that models also provide a distinctive form of intellectual satisfaction which the scientist values.[9]

Several words of caution are needed, however. The 'intuitive intelligibility' of a model is no guarantee at all concerning its validity; deductions from the theory to which the model leads must be *carefully tested against the data* and, more often than not, the proposed model must be amended or discarded. Models are not advanced as guaranteed truths; they are used to generate plausible hypotheses to investigate. They are a source of promising theories to test. Again, a model need not be picturable, though it must be conceivable, in both science and religion. Visualizable features may be selectively suppressed, as when we imagine colourless elastic spheres. In quantum physics mechanical models are given up and there are severe limitations on the use of visualizable models. In a later chapter I will maintain, nevertheless, that even in quantum physics there are models with the three characteristics I have mentioned – models which are analogical, extensible and intelligible as units.

2. THE STATUS OF MODELS

What is the relation between theoretical models and the world? There have been four alternative views of the status of *models*, and each has been closely associated with a particular view of the status of *theories*:

1. *Naive realism.* With a few exceptions, most scientists until the present century assumed that scientific theories were accurate descriptions of 'the world as it is in itself'. The entities postulated in theories were believed to exist, even if they were not directly observable. Theoretical terms were said to denote real things of the same kind as physical objects in the perceived world. Theoretical statements were understood as true or false propositions about actual entities (atoms, molecules, genes, etc.). The main difficulty with

naive realism is that we have no access to 'the world in itself', especially in the sub-microscopic domain; there is no way to compare a theory directly with 'reality'. Moreover, theoretical concepts are not given to us by nature; they are mental constructs, and often are only very remotely connected with observations. The history of science does not show the kind of simple convergence and cumulation which naive realism would lead one to expect; instead, there have been radical conceptual changes and paradigm shifts, as we will see in Chapter 6 below.

Corresponding to a naively realistic view of theories is *a literalistic view of models*. Models were taken as replicas of the world, 'pictures of reality'. Lord Kelvin said in 1884: 'I never satisfy myself until I can make a mechanical model of a thing. If I can make a mechanical model I can understand it.'[10] But such literalism always runs the risk that one will push an analogy too far and neglect important differences between the new situation and the familiar analogue. Thus the analogy between light waves and sound waves, which was so fruitful at one stage in the history of science, led to the erroneous assumption that light, like sound, must be transmitted through a medium (the hypothetical 'aether'). The nineteenth-century predilection for picturable mechanical models has been thoroughly undermined by quantum physics which has shown that the atomic world is very unlike the world of familiar objects.

2. *Positivism*. To the early positivists, a theory is a summary of data, a formula for giving a resumé of experience. Theoretical concepts are merely convenient categories for classifying observations. In British thought there has been a strong empiricist tradition, going back to Bacon, Hume, and Mill, which has emphasized the observational side of science. When physicists in the early twentieth century used concepts further and further removed from observations, positivist philosophers of science, such as Bridgman and Carnap, looked on these abstract concepts as purely mathematical symbols for correlating observations. They wanted to accept only theoretical terms which could be 'operationally defined' in observational terms; they claimed that all theoretical statements should be exhaustively translatable into observation statements.[11]

However, positivists were unable to carry out in practice their programme for translating theoretical into observational statements. It was realized also that scientific progress would be hindered if their programme could be achieved, since the extensibility of a theory arises from its application to new situations. A theory may be relevant to an indefinite number of new kinds of observation. We will also see in Chapter 6 that the scientist never has the bare data, uninterpreted by theory, which positivists sought; there is no neutral observation-language, since 'all data are theory-laden'.

Positivists have usually *dismissed models* and held that theories can be inferred directly from observations by a process of inductive generalization. (In the diagram above, they want to keep only the right column, and both the model of 'tiny elastic spheres' and the analogy with billiard-balls would be omitted; the double arrow of inference would have to point upward to represent the induction of theory from data, rather than downward to represent the deduction of expected observations from theory.) I have argued, on the contrary, that models often play an essential part in the origins and continued development of scientific theories. Theories are the product of creative imagination, often mediated through models, and not the result of simply generalizing from the data.

3. *Instrumentalism.* Instrumentalists agree with positivists that theories are not representations of the world. They hold that theories should not be judged by truth or falsity, but by their usefulness as calculating devices for correlating observations and making predictions. Toulmin calls theories 'techniques for making inferences', whereby experimental predictions can be made from initial observations.[12] Theories are also organizing guides for directing research and practical tools for technical control. Unlike positivists, however, instrumentalists acknowledge that theories are the product of man's creative imagination. They maintain, moreover, that theoretical terms cannot be exhaustively translated into equivalent observation terms. Theoretical terms are not eliminable, and the most powerful concepts may have no direct correspondence to observation terms.

The corresponding instrumentalist view of models can be called *fictionalism.* It is said that models, too, are neither true nor false, but only more or less useful mental devices. They are regarded as temporary psychological aids in setting up theoretical equations; having served their purpose, they should be discarded. (One would start, as in the diagram above, with a model leading to a theory, and the deductive arrow would point downward from theory to data; but once one had the theory, the model would be erased as superfluous.) Models are 'disreputable understudies for mathematical formulas', or in Duhem's words, 'props for feeble minds'.[13] Even the more cautious instrumentalists, such as Richard Braithwaite, consider models to be dispensable; they are only 'a convenient way of thinking about the structure of the theory'.[14] Braithwaite urges us to avoid all reference to such unobservable entities as elastic particles. I will examine this view in the following section.

4. *Critical realism.* Like the naive realist (and unlike the instrumentalist), the critical realist takes theories to be representations of the world. He holds that valid theories aretrue as well as useful. To him, science is discovery and exploration as well as construction and invention. The scientist, he insists, seeks to understand and not just to predict or control. Unlike the naive realist, however, the critical realist (along with the instrumentalist) recognizes the importance of human imagination in the formation of theories. He acknowledges the incomplete and selective character of scientific theories. Theories, in short, are abstract symbol systems which inadequately represent particular aspects of the world for specific purposes. The critical realist thus tries to acknowledge both the creativity of man's mind and the existence of patterns in events not created by man's mind. Descriptions of nature are human constructions but nature is such as to bear description in some ways and not others. No theory is an exact account of the world, but some theories agree with observations better than others because the world has an objective form of its own.[15]

I will be defending a *critical realism concerning theoretical models*, a position between literalism at the one extreme and fictionalism at the other. Let us grant that a model is a mental construct and not a picture of reality. It is an attempt to represent symbolically, for restricted purposes, aspects of a world whose structure is not accessible to us. No direct comparison of model and world is possible. But let us preserve the scientist's realistic intent in his use of theoretical models. The extension of theories seems to require that models and the questions they suggest be assigned a more important status than instrumentalism allows. The scientist today usually takes his models *seriously but not literally*. Models are limited and inadequate ways of imagining what is not observable. They remain hypothetical; gases behave *as if* they were composed of tiny elastic spheres. The 'as if' reflects both a partial resemblance and a tentative commitment.[16] Leonard Nash puts it thus:

> We must not then take a theoretic model too literally; indeed *we may err by taking the model too literally*. But, as we would realize the full heuristic power inherent in it, *we must take the model very seriously*. . . . If our models are to lead us to ask, and seek answers for, new questions about the world, we must regard them as something more than 'logical superfluities', 'illicit attempts at explanation', 'convenient fictions', or the like. The lesson of scientific history is unmistakable. To the hypothetical entities sketched by our theories we must venture at least provisional grants of ontologic status. Major discoveries are made when invisible atoms, electrons, nuclei, viruses, vitamins, hormones, and genes are regarded as *existing*.[17]

3. MODELS AS USEFUL FICTIONS

Of the four positions outlined above, naive realism and positivism have few defenders today. Instrumentalism has many adherents and merits detailed discussion. It is also of interest here because it closely parallels the claim that models in religion are 'useful fictions'. This phrase, once more, is not meant to imply reference to what is known to be false. It is not like a 'fictitious name', which is a kind of deliberate deception. Nor is it like a 'legal fiction' (e.g., that a corporation is a person), which a court treats as if it were true, though it is known to be false. A 'useful fiction' is a mental construct used instrumentally for particular purposes but not assumed to be either true or false. In this section I will try to analyse the instrumentalist position with a minimum of technical terminology, but the reader who finds the argument difficult to follow could proceed to the following section.

To Braithwaite, a scientific model is *a temporary psychological aid* in the formation of a theory. The model is dispensable once the theory has been elaborated; it is a 'heuristic device' and not in any sense a representation of reality.[18] Braithwaite holds that the ideal scientific theory has only two components: an *abstract calculus* (that is, a set of axioms and derived equations whose terms are uninterpreted mathematical symbols) and a set of *rules of correspondence* relating some of these abstract symbols to observation terms. The postulates of the theory may originally have been embedded in a model, but they should be separated from it and stated as formal axioms. The theoretical terms of the calculus obtain their meaning indirectly from the observation terms and not from the model. There are, in this view, two interpretations of the abstract calculus of the Kinetic Theory: the initial interpretation in terms of imaginary elastic spheres, which can be ignored once the theory is worked out, and the subsequent interpretation in terms of observable pressures and volumes, which remain scientifically significant.

Now it seems to me that the instrumentalist account can be criticized in regard to each of the three characteristics of models mentioned earlier. First, by stressing mathematical isomorphism it gives prominence to formal analogies and *neglects substantive analogies*. But there have been many historical cases in which rules of correspondence were suggested by analogies between observations. Thus parallels between the brightness of light and the loudness of sound, and between the colour of light and the pitch of sound, gave the clues for applying a wave theory to light when a wave theory of sound was already familiar.[19] As Achinstein points out, physical similarities in some features of a pair of situations provide grounds for the plausibility of investigating possible similarities in other features.[20] More typically, however, the substantive analogy is not observed but postulated, as when the physical properties of inertia and elasticity were attributed to the unobservable gas particles. Several recent articles have asserted that models have implicit substructures and complex associations lacking in the equations of the theory but essential to the continued growth of science.[21]

Second, having eliminated models, the instrumentalist *seems unable to provide adequately for the extension of theories.* Neither an uninterpreted formalism nor previous rules of correspondence give any clue as to possible new rules of correspondence or extensions to new types of observation. Moreover, a theory can be applied to a new domain only if, contrary to the instrumentalist thesis, its theoretical terms *do* preserve their meaning when new correspondence rules are formulated. The meaning of the theoretical terms comes from the model, not from the observation terms. It was precisely the concepts of mass and velocity, occurring originally in the theory of mechanics and attributed to the hypothetical gas particles, which suggested possible correlations with very different observation terms in the study of viscosity, or in Einstein's explanation of the 'Brownian movement'. The concept of particle velocity also suggested further novel experiments, such as those with molecular beams. What occurred was not a change of meaning but a new way of testing relations among terms with unchanged meanings – velocity, in this case. Or take the concepts of mass: we can talk about the mass of a billiard ball, or the mass of a gas particle, or the mass of the moon, precisely because the concept of mass is *not* uniquely tied to any particular type of observation.[22]

Third, the instrumentalist tends to neglect the importance of models because he is *not concerned about the process of discovery.* He pictures scientific theories as completed formal systems, and considers models to be of merely historical or psychological rather than logical interest. This seems a rather static view of science – a logician's ideal, perhaps, but one which can say nothing about the way theories originate or the way science actually develops. Scientists themselves seem to have little interest in setting up formalized axiomatic systems; there are in fact few, if any, clear examples of theories which have been completely axiomatized. There is no reason to think that scientific progress would be furthered if its concepts were replaced by bare uninterpreted symbols.

Furthermore, most instrumentalists hold that the goal of science is prediction – which is achieved by equations (interpreted calculi) rather than by models. Their claim is that *explanation is equivalent to prediction;* to explain an event, they say, is to subsume it under a law, which is equivalent to showing that the event could have been predicted from knowledge of the law and the boundary conditions.[23] This thesis has come under considerable recent criticism.[24] Toulmin has departed from his earlier instrumentalism; he now holds that theories and models have explanatory force because of the intelligibility and generality of their ideas; they yield a type of understanding which even the most accurate prediction-formula lacks.[25] He cites the fact that the Babylonians could predict eclipses with precision from time-series tables but could offer no reasons for their occurrence. This is too complex an issue to discuss here, but I would submit that if understanding rather than prediction is the goal of science, models cannot be replaced by predictive mathematical formalisms.

In addition, models contribute to *the unity of knowledge*. The presence of analogies in the structures of two or more theories promotes systematic integration and the linking of widely divergent domains. Nagel writes:

Models also contribute to the achievement of inclusive systems of explanation. A theory that is articulated in the light of a familiar model resembles in important ways the laws or theories which are assumed to hold for the model itself; and in consequence the new theory is not only assimilated to what is already familiar, but can often be viewed as an extension and generalization of an older theory which had a more limited scope. From this perspective an analogy between an old and a new theory is not simply an aid in exploiting the latter, but is a desideratum which many scientists tacitly seek to achieve in the construction of explanatory systems.[26]

Nagel grants to models a continuing and irreplaceable role in the coherent extension and unification of scientific explanations. He does not treat them as temporary expedients which should be eliminated as soon as possible, but accords them an enduring and significant role in scientific thought.

Now a reformulated instrumentalism which acknowledges an enduring and significant role for models and which remains open and non-committal concerning their ontological status, is very close to critical realism. However, I would argue that critical realism provides a logical justification, lacking in instrumentalism, for the continuing role of models. Moreover critical realism is consonant with the scientist's *quest for coherence*. Instrumentalism can offer no objection to the employment of two contradictory theories or two inconsistent models if both are useful. Yet scientists do seek coherence, even when they are aware that they have not achieved it. Often they use a plurality of models, but they do not see them as unrelated to each other, and new discoveries have arisen from attempts to resolve conflicting theories. Even the use of complementary models in quantum physics (Chapter 5) does not negate this quest for coherence.

Finally, I will suggest in Section 5 below that scientists do actually view some kinds of models as making *a tentative ontological claim* of the sort which critical realism defends. Scientists are motivated by the desire to know and understand, and not simply to predict and control. They consider theories and models as making tentative truth-claims, beyond their usefulness as tools for classifying phenomena. In particular, they hold that there are entities in the world something like those described in the model; they believe there is some isomorphism between the model and the real structures of the world.

4. METAPHORS AND MODELS

Scientific models seem far removed from literary metaphors. Yet there are some interesting parallels which warrant brief comment. In the previous chapter, I stated that a metaphor proposes analogies between the familiar context of a word and a new context into which it is introduced. There is a tension between affirmation and denial; in other words, both positive and negative analogy are present. For metaphors, as for models, it is the *neutral analogy* which invites exploration, and which prevents reduction to a set of equivalent literal statements. Metaphors were seen to be irreducible because they are open-ended.

I cited Max Black's view of metaphor as the selective transfer of some of the familiar associations of a word; certain features of the new situation are emphasized and others ignored. The sentence

'Man is a wolf' leads us to construe man as wolf-like; metaphor, in general, encourages us 'to construe one situation in terms of another'. Black goes on to propose that scientific models are *systematically-developed metaphors*. A model suggests new ways of looking at a problematical situation by transferring some of the features of another situation which is better understood. 'It may help us to notice what would otherwise be overlooked and to shift the relative emphasis attached to details – in short, to see new connections.'[27] Black stresses the role of imagination in both the sciences and the humanities. Hesse follows Black and speaks of theoretical explanation in science as 'metaphoric re-description'. She notes that neither metaphor nor model is private or merely subjective in its use, since in both cases the ideas and implications associated with the familiar domain are shared by a community of language users:

> Acceptance of the view that metaphors are meant to be intelligible implies rejection of all views that make metaphor a wholly noncognitive, subjective, emotive, or stylistic use of language. There are exactly parallel views of scientific models that have been held by many contemporary philosophers of science, namely, that models are purely subjective, psychological, and adopted by individuals for private heuristic purposes. But this is wholly to misdescribe their function in science. Models, like metaphors, are intended to communicate. If some theorist develops a theory in terms of a model, he does not regard it as a private language, but presents it as an ingredient of his theory.[28]

Donald Schon has also given a protracted comparison of models and metaphors. He holds that both offer *programmes for exploring* new situations. Neither models nor metaphors subsume analogous situations under general concepts already formulated; instead, they both intimate a similarity not yet fully conceptualized. One is asked, as it were, to find features of the old in the new; one is offered new ways of looking at a phenomenon.[29] Harré has pointed out that many scientific terms are themselves metaphorical and carry an important component of meaning from their original context. Electrical 'current', for example, is not simply defined by ammeter readings but carries an implicit reference to the current in a river. Such 'picture-carrying expressions', he says, are essential for the growth of science, and without them 'the theory would lead nowhere':

They carry the picture with which everyone, schoolboy, student, engineer and research worker, operates in dealing with problems in his field. You may deny that you have a model and be as positivistic as you like, but while the standard expressions continue to be used you cannot but have a picture. [30]

Even an analogy which was not essential to the formulation of a theory can influence its future development – as, for example, when molecular biologists speak of the genetic 'code' of DNA molecules in terms of 'letters', 'words', 'sentences', and 'punctuation'.

We will note later that in science there is no sharp line separating *theoretical* language from *observational* language; the distinction is relative, shifting, and context-dependent. All observation-reports are theory-laden; the theoretical framework influences what is taken to be 'data'. There is a close parallel in the interaction of *metaphorical* language and *literal* language; there is no sharp line between the two, but only a distinction which is relative, shifting, and context-dependent.[31] 'Man is a wolf' invites reflection not only on wolf-life characteristics of man, but also on man-like characteristics of the wolf, which is seen thereafter as more human. Again, a term initially introduced metaphorically (e.g. 'foothill' or 'skyscraper') may come to be used as a standard word and the original analogy is forgotten. Metaphors, like models, influence the supposedly literal reporting of facts, and they extend language by the creation of new meanings.

I do not, of course, intend to equate metaphors and models. A metaphor evokes many types of personal experience, including emotional and valuational responses. A scientific model, on the other hand, is *systematically developed*, and the positive and negative analogy are specified, even though the neutral analogy remains open for further exploration. Above all, scientific models lead to *theories* which can be tested experimentally (Chapter 6 below). Nevertheless there are enough similarities between metaphors and models to illustrate the importance of analogical imagination in very diverse fields of human thought. Although metaphors are not literally true, they do, in Wheelwright's words, 'say something, however tentatively and obliquely, about the nature of what is'. They can help to illustrate for us the range of alternatives which lie between literalism and fictionalism.

5. THE FUNCTIONS OF SCIENTIFIC MODELS

I will conclude by noting again the variety of types of model in science and trying to specify those to which the position of critical realism might be applicable. Recall that in broadest terms the function of models is the ordering of experience and that within science this may involve a wide diversity of specific types of activity. I mentioned *experimental models*, such as wind-tunnel models of proposed airplane designs, which are used to obtain approximate solutions to practical problems when it is difficult to experiment on the primary system. *Mathematical models*, such as the equations for the growth of a population of insects, are used to make quantitative predictions of particular variables. *Computer models* can be used to carry out calculations with many variables among which specifiable relationships are assumed, and can thereby simulate the behaviour of quantifiable aspects of such complex systems as urban transportation networks. These 'simulation models' are prominent in the new fields of 'operations research' and 'systems analysis'. They are heuristic aids in problem-solving.

Sometimes the same mathematical model is applicable to two different kinds of physical system, and one system is said to be a model of the other. These can be called '*formal analogues*', since there are two quite distinct physical domains which could never be confused with each other. For instance, the same second-order differential equation is applicable to the vibratory oscillations of a pendulum, an electric circuit, and a violin string, but neither the observable variables nor the theoretical concepts have anything else in common. Mathieu's equation occurs in analysis of the motion of an elliptical membrane and of the equilibrium of an acrobat – but there the resemblance ends. Any analogy is purely formal; there are no parallels beyond this mathematical isomorphism. The only point of the comparison is to make use of familiar mathematical procedures in computation.

Some models embodying formal analogies were indeed introduced as *deliberate fictions*. Maxwell, for instance, showed that the equations of an electric field would be the same as those for the flow of 'an imaginary incompressible fluid'; the purpose of invoking the latter was 'to make the mathematical theorems more intelligible to certain minds'.[32] At least in his early work he seems to have regarded the incompressible fluid and the electric field as analogues whose only resemblance is mathematical isomorphism. Even when there is no explicit disclaimer of the status of the model, the scientist usually knows when he is introducing it as an imaginary construct which is not intended to represent the world. I would want to distinguish these cases from theoretical models which the scientist usually views more realistically.

The character of a scientist's commitment to a *theoretical model* may vary widely in the course of its history. When it is first introduced, it may be used very tentatively for very limited purposes, correlating a narrow range of phenomena. But the scientist tries to develop a consistent model covering as many aspects of the phenomena as possible. As the scope and reliability of theories to which the model leads increases, his confidence in it also increases. In the process, the model may be altered considerably; we saw that the model of gas particles came to include features such as mutual attraction which are not found at all in billiard balls. The model becomes more complex, and draws from many other analogies besides the initial one. The original model may still be employed as a useful approximation, but it is then recognized as a deliberate simplification.

To complete the earlier example, we should recall that the 'elastic spheres' were identified with the *hypothetical molecules* which Gay-Lussac had posited from experiments on the combining volumes of chemically active gases. The search for such models linking two sciences having quite different observation terms would not be encouraged by the fictionalist position. In the present century, models of molecules have not been abandoned but have undergone further modification under the impact of quantum physics, as we shall see later. Many analogies besides those with billiard balls have contributed to the more recent models of a gas particle. The quantum physicist Max Born has written: 'All great discoveries in experimental physics have been due to the intuition of men who made free use of models which were for them not products of the imagination but representatives of real things.'[33]

But there is a wide variety even among *theoretical models*. Some, such as the 'double-helix' model of the DNA molecule, are closer to observations and can be taken more literally. Yet even in these cases one must remember that only certain aspects of the world are brought into prominence by the model, while other aspects are neglected (e.g., the model represents spatial relationships among the DNA components but not the character of the bonds between them). Other models, such as the abstract psi-functions of quantum physics, seem to invite a fictionalist interpretation. Yet even in that case there is a referential intent and a necessity of experimentation which are not present in pure mathematics. Most physicists hold that electrons exist, even though they are not waves or particles. Perhaps some biologists verge on literalism and some physicists verge on fictionalism, but the majority of practicing scientists are probably closer to the intermediate position which I have called critical realism.

Critical realism recognizes that models are selective; they allow us to deal with only restricted aspects of events. Entities in the world are assumed to be two stages removed from the familiar systems on which the model is based: (1) gas molecules are *not* the 'tiny elastic spheres' of the model (if we are not naive realists), and (2) 'tiny elastic spheres' are *not* billiard balls (if we have kept negative analogy in mind). The critical realist makes only a tentative commitment to the existence of entities something like those portrayed in the model. He says that gas molecules exist, and are in some ways like tiny elastic spheres – or, he would now say, like the wave and particle models of quantum physics.

Let me summarize the main themes of his chapter. First, models have a variety of uses in science. They serve diverse functions, some practical and some theoretical. Second, theoretical models are novel mental constructions. They originate in a combination of analogy to the familiar and creative imagination in inventing the new. They are open-ended, extensible, and suggestive of new hypotheses. Third, such models are taken seriously but not literally. They are neither pictures of reality nor useful fictions; they are partial and inadequate ways of imagining what is not observable.

4

Models in Religion

———————

ONE OF THE functions of models in science is to suggest theories which correlate patterns in observational data. One of the functions of models in religion, I submit, is to suggest beliefs which correlate patterns in human experience. The testing of scientific theories and the corresponding testing of religious beliefs are the topics of subsequent chapters. In this chapter I will propose that the character of religious models is in several respects similar to that of scientific models. First, religious models are *analogical*. The analogical basis of metaphor, symbol and parable were outlined in Chapter 2 above. The role of analogy in the more systematically-developed interpretive images which we have called models must now be examined.

Models in religion are also *extensible* and *unitary*. I stated in Chapter 2 above that models can represent the enduring structures of the cosmic order which myths dramatize in narrative form. Images which originated in religious experience and key historical events are extended to interpret other areas of individual and corporate experience. As models of an unobservable gas molecule are later used to interpret other patterns of observation in the laboratory, so models of an unobservable God are used to interpret new patterns of experience in human life. Ultimate interpretive models – whether of a personal God or of an impersonal cosmic process – are organizing images which restructure one's perception of the world. One may notice features which might otherwise have been ignored. Moreover, religious models are readily grasped as unitary wholes. Because of their vividness and immediacy, they are strongly evocative of personal response, but they also help to integrate the interpretation of diverse areas of experience.

I will argue that religious models, like scientific ones, should be taken seriously but not literally. On the one hand, they are *not literal pictures of reality*. In the biblical tradition the limitations of models are recognized. The prohibition of graven images 'or any likeness' (Ex.20.4) is both a rejection of idolatry and an acknowledgment that God cannot be adequately represented in visual imagery. 'His ways are not our ways', for he is 'beyond our farthest thought'. Perhaps with auditory symbols (e.g. 'the Word', 'the voice of the Lord') one is less tempted to think one can visualize God. In any case, biblical language is reticent about claiming to describe God as he is in himself, though it uses models freely. The creative theologian, like the creative scientist, realizes that his models are not exhaustive descriptions. Neither God nor a gas molecule can be pictured. An additional safeguard against literalism is provided by the sense of awe and mystery associated with religious experience.

But if we insist that religious models are not literal descriptions, can we avoid the opposite extreme of treating them as *useful fictions*? Braithwaite, who considers scientific models dispensable, in turn treats religious language as a morally useful fiction. Its function is to express and evoke distinctive ethical attitudes. Stories about God, he says, are parables whose only point is to recommend attitudes. We don't ask whether they are true or false but how they are used. Parables are imaginative ways of endorsing an ethical policy or affirming one's commitment to a pattern of life. They are declarations of one's intention to act in a particular way – with unselfish love, for example. A model of God, on this reading, would be a psychologically helpful fiction which supports moral behaviour. Braithwaite's instrumentalism is discussed in Section 2 below.

In addition to these questions concerning the status of religious models, this chapter asks about the *diversity of functions* which they serve. I indicated earlier that historians and anthropologists have delineated the variety of tasks which myths perform in human life. Contemporary philosophers have also shown some of the varied ways in which religious language is used. Sometimes it does, as

Braithwaite says, recommend a way of life or endorse a set of moral principles. Again, it may express and evoke a distinctive self-commitment. It may propose a particular kind of self-understanding or engender a characteristic set of attitudes towards human existence. It produces, that is, a typical form of personal life-orientation. Religious language may also express gratitude, dependence and worship. These are all functions very different from any of the functions of scientific language. Another proposed role for religious models, the evocation of 'disclosures', has been presented by Ian Ramsey; I have given in Section 3 below a critique of his scheme.

But beyond all these non-cognitive uses, I will maintain that a religious model may also direct attention to particular patterns in events. It provides a perspective on the world and an *interpretation of history and human experience*. In particular, religious models are used in the interpretation of distinctive kinds of experience, such as awe and reverence, mystical joy, moral obligation, reorientation and reconciliation, and key historical events. An even wider scope has been claimed for 'metaphysical models', concerning which I will express some reservations in Section 4 below. In subsequent chapters the crucial problems of verification, falsification, and the testing of the beliefs derived from models, will be taken up.

1. MODELS IN THE INTERPRETATION OF EXPERIENCE

In the previous chapter I mentioned Black's contention that both metaphors and models involve '*construing as*' (e.g. construing man as a wolf, or construing a gas as a collection of tiny elastic spheres). I would like now to set forth Wisdom's idea of '*seeing as*', Hick's idea of '*experiencing as*', and the idea I would favour, '*interpreting as*'. I will take these three phrases to represent alternative renditions of the way models are used in the interpretation of experience.

The point of departure must be the page of Wittgenstein's *Philosophical Investigations* on which appears a famous sketch which can be seen as a rabbit or as a duck.[1] Wittgenstein says that we do not simply see; we '*see as*', interpreting according to a pattern. John Wisdom applies the phrase to the world in its totality, which can be seen in more than one way. He tells a now-classic parable about two men who return to their long-neglected garden, in which both flowers and weeds are growing. One man is convinced that 'some gardener must tend this plot'; he points to evidence supporting his view. The other is sure that there is no gardener, and points out opposing evidence. Similarly throughout their lives, people use 'models with which to get the hang of the patterns in the flux of experience'.[2]

Later comments by Flew and others on Wisdom's parable have dwelt on one point in it: the two men do not differ concerning the facts about the garden. But Wisdom himself went on to say they do differ concerning their interpretations, and that the difference is significant and discussable. Each can try to help the other person to see the garden as he himself does by *drawing attention to certain patterns* among the facts, by connecting them up in distinctive ways and by mentioning features which might have been overlooked. Like a judge trying to decide in a law court whether there was negligence in a controversial case, the men in the parable must weigh the cumulative effect of many factors. 'Reasons for and against may be offered.' The men differ not simply in attitudes but in beliefs. 'It seems to me', writes Wisdom, 'that some belief as to what the world is like is of the essence of religion.'[3] Religious models, then, serve an 'attention-directing' function, accentuating the patterns which we see in the facts.

John Hick develops the idea of 'seeing as' a step further into *'experiencing as'*, in which there is a greater involvement of the total person. Someone might say, 'In the twilight I experienced the tuft of grass as a rabbit.' All experience, says Hick, is 'experiencing as'. To recognize an object as a fork is 'to experience it in terms of a concept', rather than to receive it as a bare observation. So religious faith, Hick proposes, consists in 'experiencing life as encounter with God':

The Old Testament prophets, for example, experienced their historical situation as one in which they were living under the sovereign claim of God, and in which the appropriate way for them to act was as God's agents . . . It is important to appreciate that this was not an interpretation in the sense of a theory imposed retrospectively upon remembered facts. It was the way in which the prophet actually experienced and participated in these events at the time. He consciously lived in the situation experienced in this way.[4]

According to Hick, *experiencing* life *as* encounter with God involves one's whole person and transforms one's total life. It leads one to act in terms of the interpreted experience. 'All of life is for him a dialogue with the divine *Thou*; in and through all his dealings with life he is having to do with God.' Yet Hick also insists that there is considerable ambiguity in the given. 'What we can know depends in consequence, to an important extent, upon what we choose to be and to do.' God safeguards our freedom by leaving room for more than one interpretation. The need for 'a voluntary act of interpretation' and 'a freely offered response' protects man from total domination by God.[5]

Although I agree with Hick's general position, it seems to me preferable to use the expression *'interpreting as'* rather than 'experiencing as'. In Hick's example, I would say 'I interpreted the tuft of grass as a rabbit', acknowledging that I had misinterpreted it (whereas it would seem strange to say that I misexperienced it). Similarly a man converted from theism to atheism would probably say that he had previously misinterpreted his experience. Hick's phrase is perhaps more appropriate for the unselfconscious experience of biblical man than for the reflective outlook of a person today who is aware of a plurality of interpretive frameworks. But my phrase differs from his only in emphasis, since he also acknowledges that there is no sharp line between experience and interpretation. We cannot isolate uninterpreted experience.

We can, however, reflect on the *distinctive types of experience* which have been most prominent in religion and try to describe them without explicit reference to any particular religious interpretation. The first two are discussed in detail in the next chapter, the others in subsequent chapters:

1. *Awe and reverence.* Men in many cultures have described a sense of mystery and wonder, holiness and sacredness, in a variety of contexts. Rudolf Otto's classic study finds in numinous experience a combination of fascination and dread. Often there seems to be a

sense of otherness, confrontation and encounter, or of being grasped and laid hold of. Correspondingly, man is aware of his own dependence, finitude, limitation and contingency.[6]

2. *Mystical union.* The mystics of many religious traditions have spoken of the experience of the unity of all things. Unity is found in the depth of the individual soul and in the world of nature. It is achieved in the discipline of meditation and is characterized by joy, harmony, serenity and peace. In its extreme form, the unity may be described as a loss of individuality and the joy as bliss or rapture.

3. *Moral obligation.* Decisions on ethical questions sometimes demand an inescapable responsibility and the subordination of one's own inclinations. Though the voice of conscience is in part the product of social conditioning, it apparently is not entirely so; it may lead a person to express judgment on his culture and to oppose his society even at the risk of death. According to Peter Berger, moral outrage in the face of evil, courage in defiance of death, and trust in an underlying cosmic order are among the 'prototypical human gestures' which can be interpreted as 'signals of transcendence'. Donald Evans holds that indignant compassion and courage in spite of anxiety are depth experiences which can be interpreted as revelations of God. When men fail to respond to moral demands they experience guilt.[7]

4. *Reorientation and reconciliation.* In individual life, acknowledgment of guilt and repentance may be followed by the experience of forgiveness. Persons unable to accept themselves are somehow enabled to do so. Such reorientation may lead to a new freedom from anxiety, an openness to new possibilities in one's life, a greater sensitivity to other persons. Grace is experienced in the healing power of love at work in our midst when reconciliation overcomes estrangement.[8]

5. *Interpersonal relationships.* The interaction between two persons is sometimes characterized by directness, immediacy, mutuality and genuine dialogue. In an 'I-Thou' relationship, as Martin Buber describes it, there is availability, sensitivity, openness, responsibility, freedom to respond; one is totally involved as a whole person. Buber suggests that one can interpret the neighbour's need as a

divine summons. Encounter with the human Thou is a form of encounter with the eternal Thou. One understands oneself to be addressed through events. 'The sound of which the speech consists are the events of personal every-day life.' A person replies through the speech of his life; he answers with his actions. Events in daily life can be interpreted as dialogue with God.[9]

6. *Key historical events.* In addition to individual aspects of experience, the data of religion include the corporate experience of communities which have arisen in response to historical events. Key events in the past continue to illuminate the present life of a community. In H. R. Niebuhr's words, 'such events help us understand ourselves and what has happened to us'. The message of the Hebrew prophets was an interpretation of the pattern of events in Israel's national life. The Christian community arose in response to the life of Christ, which is the continuing centre of its common memory. Every community celebrates and re-enacts particular historical events which are crucial to its corporate identity and its vision of reality.[10]

7. *Order and creativity in the world.* The teleological argument has been debated by philosophers from Aristotle and Aquinas to Hume and Kant, continuing into the present century. It has not, however, been as prominent in the actual life and thought of religious communities – even in the eighteenth and early nineteenth centuries, when the argument from design was frequently presented by Christian apologists. Yet it cannot be denied that many persons have been impressed by the order and beauty of the world, the intricate complexity and interdependence of natural forms; a response of wonder in confronting nature is not confined to primitive man. In their reflective moments, many men have speculated about the ultimate ground of order and creativity in the cosmic process.[11]

Now each of these seven very diverse areas of experience is subject to *a variety of interpretations.* Cultural presuppositions condition all interpretive categories. Interpretation influences experience, as will be stressed in later chapters. I am not claiming that moral and religious experience or particular historical events can constitute a proof for the existence of a personal God. I am only saying that it is reasonable to interpret them theistically and that it makes a difference whether one does so or not. It makes a difference not only in one's attitudes and behaviour but in the way one sees the world. One may notice and value features of individual and corporate life which one otherwise might have overlooked. Construing the world through a model of ultimate purpose unifies a diversity of experiences, for the same power is understood to be at work in all of them.

A variety of *analogies* has been used in the interpretation of the *corporate* experience of communities. Israel understood the pattern of events in her national life as the working out of a divine convenant analogous to the covenant agreements familiar in the ancient world. Historical situations were interpreted by the prophets in relation to an image of God and his purposes for the nation. In the prophetic literature, various specific kinds of familiar person are the analogues for images of God as King, Judge, Shepherd, Husband, Father, etc. In biblical religion, these various images form a model of God as a personal being, which is used in interpreting corporate as well as individual experience.

Through such a model, in short, characteristic areas of experience, such as those listed above, are interpreted as manifestations of God. 'Interpreting as' is very much like 'construing as' discussed in previous chapters. We can take it to include 'seeing as', as a special case, since interpretation includes visual interpretation. If the experiential basis is stressed, and the inseparability of experience and interpretation acknowledged, it differs only in emphasis from 'experiencing as'. Models not only direct attention to particular aspects of and patterns in experience but provide a framework within which a variety of types of experience can be integrated. A person with a theistic model will interpret his whole life as lived in the presence of God.

2. MODELS IN THE EXPRESSION OF ATTITUDES

We shall now consider some alternative views. The first of these is the instrumentalist claim that religious models are useful fictions whose function is *the expression and evocation of distinctive attitudes*. I will take attitudes to include feelings, value judgments, and policies of action. Braithwaite argues that religious assertions are 'primarily declarations of adherence to a policy of action, declarations of commitment to a way of life'.[12] Religious language is a form of moral language, an affirmation of one's intention to act in a particular way. It is prescriptive rather than descriptive. But it is not merely emotive or expressive of feelings, since policies of action are resented. In a religious tradition such a declaration of ethical policy is associated with 'stories' or 'parables' which Braithwaite treats as morally useful fictions:

> For it is not necessary, on my view, for the asserter of a religious assertion to believe in the truth of the story involved in the assertions: what is necessary is that the story should be entertained in thought. . . . Many people find it easier to resolve upon and to carry through a course of action which is contrary to their natural inclinations if this policy is associated in their minds with certain stories. And in many people the psychological link is not appreciably weakened by the fact that the story associated with the behaviour is not believed. Next to the Bible and the Prayer Book the most influential work in English Christian religious life has been a book whose stories are frankly recognized as fictitious, Bunyan's *Pilgrim's Progress*.[13]

As we have seen, the term *parable* traditionally referred to a fictitious story whose main point was the attitude it suggested (e.g. the Parable of the Good Samaritan). Braithwaite extends the term to include all references to God, since he holds that these are likewise oblique ways of recommending attitudes. One does not ask whether a parable is true or false; one asks only whether it is psychologically effective in inspiring people to adopt the policies it endorses. Since they are not believed, they need not be consistent. 'Indeed a story may provide better support for a long range policy of action if it contains inconsistencies.'[14] Parables about God, in this view, are narratives offering a kind of imaginative model which, like Braithwaite's scientific models, have the status of psychologically helpful fictions.

A similar instrumentalism in both science and religion has been espoused by T. R. Miles. In discussing the billiard-ball model he writes: 'Models of this sort are not normally shown to be true or false by crucial experiments; it is rather that they work well or badly for particular purposes, and when they work badly they gradually fall into disuse.'[15] When he turns to religious language, Miles describes a believer as a person who accepts '*the "theistic" parable* – the parable of a loving father who has called us all to be like him and to become his children'. Acceptance of the theistic parable commits us to distinctive kinds of action, but we cannot ask whether the parable is objectively valid since it is neither true nor false. Adopting it is not like trying to discover facts, but is a decision to make an act of personal commitment. 'To accept the theistic parable is to commit ourselves to a particular way of life.' All men live according to some dominant parable:

> All of us alike are confronted with the question of how we ought to live; and whatever way of life we choose, we can be said to be implicitly accepting one set of parables or another. If the parable which we accept is not that of the loving father, it is likely to be that of a purposeless world, indifferent or actively hostile to man's highest endeavours. Such a parable cannot be shown to be wrong. But to live in accordance with it involves a commitment no less than does living in accordance with the theistic parable.[16]

Now I would agree that religious language does indeed express and evoke distinctive attitudes. It does encourage self-commitment to a way of life; it acknowledges allegiance to ethical principles and affirms the intention to act in particular ways. But I would maintain that these *non-cognitive uses* presuppose *cognitive beliefs*. To be sure, religious faith is not simply assent to the truth of propositions; but it does require the assumption that certain propositions are true. It would be unreasonable to adopt or recommend a way of life unless one believes that the universe is of such a character that this way of life is appropriate. 'Useful fictions' are no longer useful if they are recognized as fictions or treated as 'parables' whose truth or falsity is taken to be irrelevant. *Pilgrim's Progress*, cited by Braithwaite, was an influential guide to behaviour only because it was read as an allegory faithfully representing the way of life recommended by the Bible and supported by the claims therein about God and the world. In addition, we should note again that religious language expresses worshipful as well as ethical attitudes, and thereby implicitly affirms an object of worship.

In Donald Evans' view, the functions of religious language are very diverse and go far beyond the support of moral behaviour. Yet for him also *the expression of attitudes* is central. He starts from a general discussion of 'self-involving language' which expresses attitudes, feelings and commitments rather than neutral facts.[17] He then asks us to consider sentences of the form 'I look on x as y'. If I say 'I look on Tories as vermin', I indicate that my attitude towards Tories is similar to my attitude towards vermin, but I give no indication of objective similarities between Tories and vermin themselves. If I say 'I look on Henry as a brother', I commit myself to treating him as a brother, even though in fact he does not act like a brother. I acknowledge similar attitudes in two situations, without specifying analogies between the situations themselves. 'Looking on' differs from 'seeing as', 'interpreting as', and other expressions mentioned earlier in this chapter, for it refers only to attitudes and policies.

So also, says Evans, scripture provides *analogies for our attitudes* towards God, rather than analogies concerning God himself. I am to 'look on God as a father'; I am to have the kind of respect and trust I ought to have towards a father, even though I cannot say in what respects God resembles a father since he is not describable. Similarly the creation story is 'a parable suggesting attitudes towards the world'. If I look on God as father, creator, etc., my resulting conduct will be appropriate.

Evans enjoins us to *adopt these attitudes* because they are recommended by scripture, not because we understand in what way they are appropriate. By appealing to revelation, he does manage to avoid treating parables as 'useful fictions', but they remain devoid of cognitive content beyond the endorsement of distinctive attitudes:

When I look on God as y, I can only specify the similarity between God and y attitudinally; I believe and hope that God is *such that* the attitude which is appropriate towards him is similar to the attitude which is appropriate towards y . . . The expression of an onlook commits me to a way of behaving and thinking, a mode of life. Moreover, such an onlook is not a case of 'Let's pretend.' I do not merely *act as if* I believed that there is a God who is like a potter (or a victor, etc.). I act in accordance with a positive belief that God *is* like a potter; but I cannot describe this likeness except by referring to human attitudes.[18]

Evans claims that biblical language is predominantly *parabolic*; once again, it is said that to accept a parable is simply to adopt the attitude it suggests. But even if such parables are taken to be revealed (rather than treated as useful fictions), can the recommended attitudes be sustained in total isolation from *specifiable beliefs* about the object of the attitudes? The appropriateness of a response surely depends on one's understanding of that to which one is responding. Does not the biblical model of God as father offer analogies for God's fatherly nature as well as for our filial stance? In the Parable of the Prodigal Son, is not the analogy between God and the forgiving father as important as that between ourselves and the two sons? In scripture, attitudes are often justified as a response to what is understood to be the case; for example, 'We love because he first loved us' (I John 4.19). Models in religion not only encourage distinctive attitudes but purport to tell us something about God, man and the world.

3. 'DISCLOSURE MODELS'

In addition to the interpretation of experience and the expression of attitudes, there is a third function of religious models, namely the evocation of disclosures, of which Ian Ramsey has been an articulate proponent. Since he has made extensive use of the idea of models, we should examine his view with care. In some passages he says that models in religion, like those in science, derive from *analogies* between observations, 'the perception of significant isomorphism'. He states, for example, that there is a resemblance between patterns in the world and patterns in the behaviour of fathers which leads to the model of God as father. But he does not develop these remarks.

Again, Ramsey says that we can test the *'empirical fit'* between a religious model and reality. 'It stands or falls according to its success (or otherwise) in harmonizing whatever events are at hand.'[19] A model 'is able to incorporate a wide range of phenomena'; it 'chimes in with the world' and is 'authenticated by reality'. Unfortunately he says nothing about the relation of models to theories, which we have seen to be essential in any testing procedure in science. Although he defends what he calls the 'empirical fit' of religious models, he grants that there can be no strict 'empirical verification' because no predictions or testable deductions can be made, and because God is a mystery which we cannot comprehend. Elsewhere he writes that a model is verified by its consequences in distinctive behaviour (e.g. the power of love) and by its ability to lead to articulations which provide 'the most comprehensive and most coherent map of the universe'.[20]

Ramsey puts his main emphasis, however, on the way models are *disclosed* in both science and religion. He calls them 'self-authenticating models in which the universe discloses itself to us'.

The contemporary use of models in science or theology – models which are not picturing models – points us back, then, to that moment of insight where along with a model there is disclosed to the scientist or the theologian that about which each is to be, in his characteristically different way, articulate.[21]

I must confess that I am rather dubious about this notion of '*disclosure models*' in either field. Ramsey is evidently impressed by the suddenness and conviction of the 'moment of insight' in scientific discovery. But is any model in science 'self-authenticating' or 'disclosed as true'? A scientific model is initially a very tentative conjecture which leads to a testable theory; it may have to be modified – or more probably discarded, for most sudden inspirations in science turn out to be useless. Ramsey's illustrations of supposedly self-authenticating disclosures in science are almost invariably taken from mathematics: one suddenly 'sees the light' in looking at a geometrical theorem; 'the penny drops' as one grasps the significance of the sum of an infinite convergent series, etc. Now in mathematics insight into the relationship among ideas may indeed be 'self-authenticating', at least within the framework of accepted axioms and rules; but in science this is not the case because one is not dealing with relationships among ideas alone.

On the religious side, Ramsey holds that models are 'occasions of *divine self-disclosure*. We are to take the model 'loving father', for example, and then imagine a 'very loving father', developing it in the direction of 'infinitely loving father'. The latter is not part of the series, but a logically different realization which 'breaks in on us' as we develop the model:

For theology (I would say) is founded in occasions of insight and disclosure when, to put it at its most general, the universe declares itself in a particular way around some group of events which thus take on a cosmic significance. These events then become, and naturally, a self-appointed model which enables us to be articulate about what has been disclosed . . . So a qualifier like 'infinite' will work on a model of human love until there dawns on us that particular kind of family resemblance between the various derivative models which reveals God – God as 'infinitely loving'. God is revealed in the cosmic disclosure which may occur at some stage as the pattern of models is developed without end, just as there may dawn on us that to which an infinite convergent series points, as its terms are endlessly developed.[22]

Ramsey stresses the *'logical oddness'* of the qualifying adjectives and sees it as a reminder that we are not talking about ordinary events.[23] The direction in which the model is to be developed is one that leads to a sense of mystery and wonder, thereby safeguarding the transcendence of God. By underscoring the inadequacy of the model Ramsey prevents it from being interpreted literally, but does he not run the risk of eroding the positive analogy completely? Are there logical reasons, rather than purely psychological ones, for the ability of some models and not others to lead to disclosures? Ramsey is not simply proposing a method of meditation or a technique for achieving an experience of enlightenment. What then is the connection between the model and the disclosure? Does the model suggest any conceptual frameworks which can be discussed apart from the moment of disclosure?

Ramsey occasionally attributes this process of disclosure or 'breaking in' to *divine initiative*:

Whether the light breaks or not is something that we ourselves cannot entirely control. We can certainly choose what seem to us the most appropriate models, we can operate what seem to us the most suitable qualifiers; we can develop what seem to us the best stories, but we can never guarantee that for a particular person the light will dawn at a particular point, or for that matter at any point in any story. Need this trouble us? Is not this only what has been meant by religious people when they have claimed that the 'initiative' in any 'disclosure' or 'revelation' must come from God?[24]

More typically Ramsey says that 'the universe discloses itself to us', which may or may not imply an initiative on the part of the universe. Most of his examples, however, seem to illustrate an act of *intuitive awareness* on man's part. Apparently it is the immediacy of the insight, rather than its suddenness, which authenticates it. That Ramsey sees religious models as leading to an intuitive awareness is suggested also by the frequent parallels he draws with self-awareness. He repeatedly cites examples of the recognition of the 'I' which is neither observed nor inferred. Language about oneself, about moral awareness, and about loyalty and self-commitment, is said to be logically similar to religious language.

In Ramsey's view, each use of a model is a separate occasion of discernment, and one does not need to seek any consistency between *diverse models*. He urges us to use as many models as possible; but we are to avoid mixing discourse deriving from different models. He tells us that when we come across apparently contradictory theological doctrines, we need only trace them back to their respective models which cannot conflict since they are used independently of each other. It seems to me that by making models instrumental to the evocation of disclosures, Ramsey bypasses the problem of their relation to each other and to anything outside man. He rightly insists that models are not literal descriptions or pictures of reality, but he does not discuss the development of a coherent set of beliefs based on the models.[25]

Are there *criteria* for evaluating religious models themselves, or are they to be judged solely by their psychological effectiveness for particular individuals in evoking disclosures? Ramsey says that one can judge models in part by their effectiveness in producing loving behaviour; this criterion, taken alone, would raise again all the problems encountered in Braithwaite's instrumentalism. We have also seen that Ramsey occasionally talks about 'empirical fit' in the use of models, but this more empirical side of his thought is not systematically set forth. As he presents them, models are to be judged more by their ability to produce personal disclosures than by their ability to order experience. Ramsey maintains that the functions of religious language are the evocation of commitment and worship, which are non-cognitive functions, and also discernment, which is presumably cognitive.[26] For Ramsey, the cognitive claims apparently rest on both divine revelation and human intuition in the moment of disclosure.

If I understand him correctly, Ramsey takes *intuition* to be a form of immediate and indubitable knowledge which is not subject to revision or correction; if it is 'self-authenticating', the problem of distinguishing genuine from spurious disclosures can never arise. It appears that for him models are occasions for moments of intuitive certainty. But do we not run the risk of being arbitrary and subjective if there is no way to tell true from false disclosures? If, instead, we said that disclosures involve the evocation of experience and its interpretation by models, we could acknowledge the possibility of misinterpretation and subject our models to critical evaluation.

4. METAPHYSICAL MODELS

A fourth and final function of religious models is the construction of metaphysical systems. This resembles the first function, the interpretation of experience, except that the scope of metaphysics is broader, its motives more speculative, and its approach more systematic. Metaphysics has traditionally been understood as the search for a coherent set of general categories for the interpretation of the whole range of human experience – scientific, religious, aesthetic, moral, etc. In metaphysical thinking, says Dorothy Emmet, a pattern of relationships drawn from one area of experience is extended to coordinate other areas. The metaphysician takes a '*co-ordinating analogy*' from some relationships he judges to be specially important and from it derives a model which can order a diversity of kinds of experience:

Such ideas share something of the character of scientific models, but whereas scientific models suggest possible patterns for the co-ordination of data of a homogeneous type, the metaphysical model has to suggest a possible pattern of co-ordination between data of different types.[27]

Emmet acknowledges the selective and partial character of metaphysics, in which judgments are influenced by cultural assumptions and individual sensitivities. She concludes that perhaps no one analogy is comprehensive enough to encompass the diversity of modern life; we may have to be content with several analogies only loosely related to each other. Stephen Pepper ascribes a similar role to metaphysical models, which he calls 'root-metaphors' (note once more the reference to metaphor). He develops five basic models and concludes that none of them should be abandoned since each illuminates certain aspects of experience.[28]

Frederick Ferré has given a careful and, in my judgment, balanced account of models in religion. He views the metaphysical use of theistic models as important but subordinate to their *practical use* in focusing values and influencing life styles. The vivid 'ultimate images' of religion provide a basis for ordering valuational commitments and orienting life and action:

> For it is without doubt the imagery of the models in theology which evoke the communal adoration, obeisance, awe, devotion, ecstacy, courage – the emotive and conative dimensions of faith that constitute it *religious faith* rather than philosophical speculation or metaphysical system-building. I am not claiming that imagery alone can support such non-cognitive elements – courage without *belief* that courage is appropriate in the situation is something less than courage! – but it is precisely because the models of faith are taken as trustworthy, that is, believed to be in some sense true, that their non-cognitive functions are possible. Towards a theory without the vividness and immediacy provided by the biblical model, however, such responses could never be expected.[29]

Ferré points out that in science, and in metaphysics considered as a speculative theory, models are ancillary to the theories into which they are developed. But in religion, and in the more existential side of metaphysics, models are more influential than theories:

> For the purposes of pure theory, a model must be subordinate to its theory and must be alterable or dispensable according to the dictates of theory; but theistic imagery is not used – even on its speculative side – for theoretical purposes alone. As long as it remains *religious* imagery, the motivation to think in its terms is overridingly practical. This is not necessarily so different, however, from the normal metaphysical situation as it may sound. Seldom, if

ever, can metaphysical models, 'visions of ultimate reality', be held entirely dispassionately. A metaphysician's view of his world and of himself, as well as his sense of order and intelligibility, is wrapped up in the conceptual model he uses.[30]

In the *metaphysical articulation* of the theistic model, as Ferré shows, various conceptual schemes have been used – for example, the categories employed by Plato, Aristotle, Whitehead, or Heidegger. Conversely, the metaphysical system adopted may lead to emphasis on particular features of the model (e.g. Platonic and Aristotelian assumptions lead to emphasis on God's changelessness, self-sufficiency and omnipotence, whereas Whiteheadian thought minimizes each of these aspects). Theistic imagery can 'suggest patterns and unity in the totality of things' by virtue of 'an appeal to personal purpose, volitional power, and moral principle as the ultimate explanatory categories'. Ferré maintains that a metaphysical system can be evaluated by criteria not unlike those used in judging scientific theories. *Coherence* refers to consistency, interconnectedness, conceptual unity and the reduction of arbitrariness and fragmentation. *Inclusiveness* refers to scope, generality and ability to integrate diverse specialized languages. *Adequacy* is a matter of relevance and applicability to experience of all kinds.

Ferré grants that these *criteria* are not at all precise and that they are often in tension with one another, but he believes they can be used to evaluate metaphysical systems. No predictions can be made from such systems, however, since their categories are very general; presumably all types of past experience have already been taken into account, and no radically new types are likely to occur in the future. The absence of prediction is a major point of distinction between metaphysical and scientific models, but in other features Ferré sees considerable similarity:

Barring this one logically inappropriate means of testing the reliability of models, the metaphors of religion lie open to evaluation along very similar lines to the models used in the sciences to represent a subject matter that lies beyond our powers of direct inspection. As organizing images through which we see ourselves and all things, the powerful images of religion should bring certain aspects of our experience into prominence, should minimize the importance of other aspects, and should throughout function to illuminate our total environment by discovering to us otherwise unnoticed parallelisms, analogies, and patterns among our data. They are reliable, and thus candidates for reasonable adoption, to the extent that our experience of life as a whole (not, remember, just specific bits and pieces of experience) is open to organization in this manner without distortion, forcing, or ill fit; and to the extent that the total account of things that they suggest is consistent, unified, and free from uninterpreted disconnections.[31]

In Chapter 7 below I will discuss the verification and falsification of metaphysical systems, and the difficulties in applying criteria for evaluating them. Such difficulties lead me to seek a role for *religious beliefs* which is less comprehensive than metaphysical synthesis. That is, religious language makes cognitive claims which go beyond practical and attitudinal uses, but such claims are more modest than those of all-inclusive metaphysical systems. The primary context of religious beliefs, I will urge, is the interpretation of distinctive types of experience. Beyond this, beliefs are indeed relevant to the interpretation of personal and social life-situations and significant events in the lives of individuals and communities. The additional task of systematizing these beliefs into a theology and relating them to metaphysical categories used to interpret a variety of other types of experience must indeed be undertaken.

But the further one has moved from *the primary domain of religious language*, the greater is the danger of imposing on other domains categories which distort their data. If, in constructing a theistic metaphysics, one's interests are predominantly speculative, the distinctively self-involving functions of religious language will be forgotten. Moreover the theologian is not interested in the detailed structures of ordinary kinds of experience as such, but rather in their relation to the events and experiences which for him have special religious significance. Thus I will consider the metaphysical function of religious models as a speculative extension of the interpretation of experiences of the sort described in Section I above, rather than as another primary function in its own right.

5. THE FUNCTIONS OF RELIGIOUS MODELS

Models are only one aspect of religion, abstracted from the total matrix of life and thought of a community; we would not expect them to perform all the tasks of religious language. Some of the characteristic functions of myths, mentioned in Chapter 2 above, are not prominent in the case of models: sociological functions in integrating a group, psychological functions in reducing anxiety, ritual functions in communal celebration. Four proposed functions of models have been outlined in the present chapter: (1) the interpretation of experience, (2) the expression of attitudes, (3) the evocation of disclosures, and (4) the construction of metaphysical systems. I have advocated that whatever is valid concerning disclosures can be subsumed under the first rubric, since disclosures involve the interpretation of experience rather than the acquisition of self-authenticating knowledge. Likewise, metaphysical systems can be considered as speculative extensions of interpretive categories which within religious language itself are applied to distinctive types of experience and key historical events. The first two functions, then, will be taken as primary for religious models.

We must not underestimate the importance of *the expression of attitudes*. Religion is, first and last, a way of life; its main interest is practical rather than theoretical. Religious models do indeed present what Braithwaite calls 'policies of action'. They have the capacity to inspire devotion, serenity, new patterns of living. Whiteley is right that 'what men seek from religious experience is not information; it is encouragement, consolation, moral balance, mystical rapture'.[32] The life-orienting and valuational power of religious images cannot be denied. But we can acknowledge these non-cognitive functions without agreeing that they are the only functions of religious models.

I have defended the role of models in *the interpretation of experience*, adopting the phrase 'interpreting as' in preference to 'seeing as' or 'experiencing as', while acknowledging the inseparability of experience and interpretation. Organizing images restructure our perceptions and alter the way we see the world; they help us notice patterns among the facts which we might otherwise have missed. Models lead to religious beliefs (see Chapter 6 below); religious traditions make assertions, as well as recommending attitudes. The critical realism which I have advocated allows models to fill *both* interpretive and expressive functions, whereas instrumentalism does not. Cognitive models can fill both cognitive and non-cognitive functions, but non-cognitive models cannot.

There are, then, several *similarities* between religious models and theoretical models in science, which can be summarized as follows. First, they share the characteristics outlined previously: they are analogical in origin, extensible to new situations, and comprehensible as units. Second, they have a similar status. Neither is a literal picture of reality, yet neither should be treated as a useful fiction. Models are partial and inadequate ways of imagining what is not observable. They are symbolic representations, for particular purposes, of aspects of reality which are not directly accessible to us. They are taken seriously but not literally. Third, the use of scientific models to order observations has some parallels in the use of religious models to order the experience of individuals and communities. Organizing images help us to structure and interpret patterns of events in personal life and in the world.

There are also important *differences* between religious and scientific models. First, religious models serve non-cognitive functions which have no parallel in science. Sometimes religious models seem to survive primarily because they serve these functions effectively. Second, religious models elicit more total personal involvement than scientific models. Religious language is indeed self-involving, as both Ramsey and Evans insist. Religion asks about the objects of man's trust and loyalty, the character of his ultimate concern, the final justification for his values. The call to decision and commitment, pointed out in the discussion of parables in Chapter 2 above, is present throughout religious language. Third, as Ferré observes, religious models appear to be more influential than the formal beliefs and doctrines derived from them, whereas scientific models are subservient to theories, even though a model may outlast a series of theories developed from it. Theories are the instrument for specifying positive and negative analogy, and for correlating observations. Religious images have a more direct relationship to experience, especially in worship, ethics, and the life of the religious community.

In later chapters, additional similarities and differences between science and religion will be evident. We will see that scientific theories influence observation, but that religious beliefs influence experience in a more problematic way. Scientific theories, while not subject to any absolute verification or falsification, can be supported or undermined by empirical evidence. We will examine the scientist's commitment to paradigms, which in both science and religion are highly resistant to falsification; but I will maintain that criteria of assessment are not totally paradigm-dependent. Distinctive features of religious commitment and its relation to critical enquiry will also need consideration. Any conclusions about religious models must await these further comparisons.

5

Complementary Models

IN THE PRECEDING chapters the functions and the status of models in science and in religion were discussed. I now wish to look more specifically at the role of complementary models in twentieth-century physics, and then at some possible parallels in religious thought. Can one continue to employ two very different models within either science or religion? Can an electron be thought of as both a wave and a particle? Can one use both personal and impersonal models of Ultimate Reality?

I. THE WAVE-PARTICLE DUALITY

We have seen that *particle* models, such as the billard-ball model, dominated the classical physics of matter. By the nineteenth century, another basic type of model, that of *waves* in continuous media, was also being employed for a different group of phenomena involving light and electromagnetism. But early in the present century a number of puzzling experiments seemed to call for the use of both *wave* and *particle* models for both types of phenomena. On the one hand, Einstein's equations for the photo-electric effect and Compton's work on photon scattering showed that light travels in discrete packets, with definite energy and momentum, behaving very much like particles. Conversely, electrons, which had always been viewed as particles, showed the spread-out interference effects characteristic of waves. Waves are continuous, extended, and interact in terms of phase; particles are discontinuous, localized, and interact in terms of momentum. There seems to be no way to combine them into one unified model.

Suppose, for example, that *a beam of electrons* is shot through two narrow slits in a metal screen and strikes a photographic film placed a few centimeters behind the screen. Each electron registers as a single tiny dot on the film; it seems to arrive as a particle, and it must presumably have gone through either one slit or the other if the charge and mass of the electron are indivisible. Yet the dots on the film fall in an interference pattern of parallel bands, which can be explained only if one assumes a wave passing through both slits.[1] This same wave-particle duality is found throughout atomic physics. 'Compromise models', such as localized wave packets, provide no general resolution of the paradox. But a unified mathematical formalism can be developed which allows the observed events to be predicted statistically. One can calculate the *probability* that an electron will strike the film at any given point. Within the calculated probability-distribution, however, the point at which a particular electron will strike is not predictable at all.

Similarly, *no unified model* of the quantum atom has been developed. The earlier 'Bohr model' of the atom could be easily visualized; particle-like electrons were thought to follow orbits around the nucleus, resembling a miniature solar system. But the atom of quantum mechanics is not picturable at all. One might try to imagine patterns of probability waves filling the space around the nucleus like some three-dimensional symphony of musical tones of incredible complexity, but the analogy would not help us much. The atom is not just inaccessible to direct observation and unimaginable in terms of sensory qualities; it cannot even be described coherently in terms of classical concepts such as space, time and causality. The domain of the very small must be radically different from the domain of everyday objects. We can describe statistically by differential equations what happens in experiments, but we cannot ascribe familiar attributes consistently to the inhabitants of the atomic world. We seem to be a long way from the familiar 'billiard ball' model of nineteenth-century physics.

In quantum physics, then, models are only remotely and inconsistently related to theories; and theories in turn have extremely indirect and in general only probabilistic connections with observations. In his work, the physicist relies on the unified *mathematical formalism* of the theory and abandons dependence on pictorial representations. He may be unhappy that the equations of his theory do not yield exact predictions about individual events; his probability-distributions reflect an indeterminacy in the simultaneous measurement of pairs of variables (such as position and momentum). But no one has devised any better alternative, and the physicist has learned to live with the theory he has. He talks about 'states' and 'operators' instead of particles or waves.

It is not surprising that the positivist finds in quantum physics support for his conviction that we should *discard all models* and treat theories as mere calculational devices for correlating observations. He urges us to give up trying to imagine what goes on between observations; in the two-slit experiment, he says, it is useless to ask what the electron was doing before it hit the film. The highly abstract mathematical formalism should be treated as a mental construct for making predictions. The equations will allow us to correlate statistically the final and initial states of specified experimental situations, which are the only things we can observe. Models are superfluous and theories are useful fictions; neither is a representation of the world.

I would myself see modern physics as a strong warning *against literalism* rather than as evidence for the absolute rejection of models. Even the apparently bare formalisms of quantum theory are not 'totally uninterpreted', for they still carry imaginative associations. These may not be pictorial in character, but they do convey analogies with other fields which are important in suggesting rules of correspondence with observable variables. Nagel states:

There is of course no question whatever that the terminology of 'particles' and 'waves' is suggestive and heuristically valuable. Nevertheless, the usefulness of this terminology must not hide from us the fact that it is employed analogically and is not to be construed literally . . . Nevertheless, there are great psychological advantages in having such models for a theory. In consequence, with such models as their objective, physicists frequently formulate the content of quantum mechanics in the language of classically conceived particles and waves, because of certain analogies between the formal structures of classical and quantum mechanics . . . Accordingly, although a satisfactory uniformly complete interpretation of quantum mechanics based on a *single* model cannot be given, the theory can be satisfactorily interpreted for *each concrete experimental situation* to which the theory is applied.[2]

The *analogies* in quantum physics contribute to the interpretation of the formalism, its extension to new domains, and its possible modification. The Schrödinger 'wave equation' cannot but remind one of the familiar second-order differential equations which apply to waves. 'When the physical model of wave-motion in a material medium had to be abandoned in physics', writes Mary Hesse, 'it left its traces in the kind of mathematics which was used, for this was still a mathematical language derived from the wave equations of fluid motion, and so, for the mathematician, it carried some of the imaginative associations of the original physical picture.'[3] Dirac's theory, she maintains, presupposes a particle analogy 'which invests the formalism with experiential relevance'; the assumption of 'holes' in postulated negative-energy states led him to predict the existence of the positron. Hutten compares such highly attenuated analogies with the lingering grin of the Cheshire cat: 'The picture of the cat has receded into the background, but, knowing that there once was a cat, we understand that the residual phenomenon may be interpreted as a grin.'[4] Even a few of the associations of waves and particles may provide useful clues concerning rules of correspondence.

Hesse notes further that the wave model's *positive analogy* is the particle model's *negative analogy*, and vice versa. Hence they do not conflict directly with each other – even though they cannot be combined into one model because there is little overlap in the positive analogies. Yet if we retained only the mathematical formalism which is derived from the two positive analogies, we would lose the two *neutral analogies* which may provide promising ideas for further exploration. Thus implicit wave and particle models are not just psychological aids for the non-mathematical layman; they are of value to the scientist for extension of the theory, postulation of new correspondence rules, and applications to new types of observation. Hesse concludes:

If we were forbidden to talk in terms of models at all, we should have no expectations at all, and we should be imprisoned for ever inside the range of our existing experiments. . . . And it is in arguing in terms of these features that the particle and wave models are still essential, supplemented by the hunches that physicists have acquired about when to argue in terms of one and when the other. The particle and wave models themselves cannot be regarded as simply descriptive of reality, but when taken together in this complicated way they can be regarded as giving us knowledge of the real world.[5]

2. THE COMPLEMENTARITY PRINCIPLE

Niels Bohr has given the most influential defense for the retention of both wave and particle models along with the recognition of their limitations. 'A complete elucidation of one and the same object', he writes, 'may require diverse points of view which defy a unique description.'[6] There are three interwoven themes in his complex discussion of complementarity. First, he shows that the more *a particular experimental arrangement* makes wave-like behaviour evident, the less evident is particle-like behaviour, and vice versa. The extreme cases of unambiguous wave and particle behaviour occur in mutually exclusive laboratory situations.[7] As one physicist puts it, you may have to use a wave model on Mondays, Wednesdays and Fridays, and a particle model on Tuesdays, Thursdays, and Saturdays. But I would point out that on some days (perhaps Sundays) you may have to use both models. The extreme cases are indeed mutually exclusive, but in a middle range features of both wave and particle seem to be manifest together in a single experiment, such as the two-slit case above; neither model is adequate, yet neither can be dispensed with. The problem goes beyond that of using different models in different experiments.

A second theme frequently mentioned by Bohr is *the interaction between subject and object* in every experiment. He states that no sharp line can be drawn between the process of observation and what is observed. We are actors and not merely spectators, and we choose the experimental tools we will employ. The measuring procedure disturbs the system to be measured. But I would still ask: can this 'influence of the observer' account for the unpredictability of observations when nothing is done to disturb the system (e.g. spontaneous nuclear disintegration, or the 'diffusion of a wave packet')? The uncertainty relationship can in fact be derived from quantum theory without any reference to 'disturbing the system'. Most of Bohr's followers no longer claim that this second thesis covers all instances of indeterminacy. In any case it would not help us understand why complementary models are needed.

On this question a third theme in Bohr's writing is more illuminating, namely his discussion of *conceptual limitations* in human understanding. Man as knower, rather than man as experimenter, is the centre of attention here. Bohr shares Kant's scepticism about the possibility of knowing the world in itself. He holds that classical concepts are 'forms of perception' imposed by man. If we try, as it were, to force nature into certain conceptual moulds, we preclude the full use of other moulds. Thus we must choose between complete causal *or* spatio-temporal descriptions, between adequate wave *or* particle models, between accurate knowledge of position *or* momentum. The more one set of concepts is used, the less can the complementary set be applied simultaneously. We have successive and incomplete complementary pictures that cannot be neatly unified. This reciprocal limitation occurs because the atomic world cannot be described in terms of classical concepts, which, according to Bohr, are the only ones available to us. I would accept this stress on the importance of the categories of understanding imposed by the knower, but I would want to attribute them less to the given structures of the mind (as in Bohr's neo-Kantian view) than to the limitations of our experience and imagination. We do not need to assume, with Bohr, that waves and particles exhaust the possible types of basic model.

Bohr himself proposes that the idea of complementarity could be *extended to other phenomena* susceptible to analysis by two kinds of model: mechanistic and organic models in biology, behaviouristic and introspective models in psychology, models of free will and determinism in philosophy, or of divine justice and divine love in theology.[8] Some authors go further and speak of the complementarity of science and religion. Thus C. A. Coulson, after explaining the wave-particle duality and Bohr's generalization of it, calls science and religion 'complementary accounts of one reality'.[9]

D. M. MacKay has defended such *extended uses* of the idea of complementarity. He defines two descriptions as complementary if (*a*) they have a common referent, (*b*) the logical preconditions for their use are mutually exclusive, and (*c*) each is in principle exhaustive in its own frame of reference. The wave-particle duality in physics is for him an instance of a more general logical relationship between two accounts of one object under differing conditions or from different perspectives. According to his definition, vertical and horizontal plans of a building are 'complementary descriptions'. So are mental and physical descriptions of a person's activity. MacKay concludes that science and religion may likewise be considered complementary.[10]

I am somewhat dubious about such extended usage of the term if it is intended to convey some parallel with complementarity in physics. I would want to set down several conditions for applying the concept of complementarity:

1. Complementarity provides *no justification for an uncritical acceptance of dichotomies*. It cannot be used to avoid dealing with inconsistencies or to veto the search for unity. The 'paradoxical' element in the wave-particle duality should not be over-emphasized. We do not say that an electron is both a wave and a particle, but that it exhibits wave-like and particle-like behaviour; moreover we do have a unified mathematical formalism which provides at least probabilistic predictions. And as Feyerabend insists, we cannot rule out in advance the search for new unifying models (such as David Bohm's postulation of sub-atomic causal mechanisms), even though previous attempts have not yielded any new theories in better agreement with the data than quantum theory.[11] Coherence remains an important ideal and criterion in all reflective enquiry.

2. Models should be called complementary only if they refer to *the same entity* and are of *the same logical type*. Wave and particle are models of a single entity (e.g. an electron) in a single situation (e.g. a two-slit experiment); they are on the same logical level and had previously been employed in the same discipline. As Peter Alexander

has pointed out, these conditions do not apply to 'science and religion'.[12] They do not refer to the same entity. They arise typically in differing situations and serve differing functions in human life. For these reasons I will speak of science and religion as alternative languages using alternative models, and restrict the term 'complementary' to models of the same logical type *within* a given language.

3. The complementarity of models, under these conditions, underscores *the inadequacy of literalism*. The use of one model limits the use of the other; they are not simply 'alternative models' having different domains or functions. They are symbolic representations of aspects of reality which cannot be consistently visualized in terms of analogies with everyday experience; they are only very indirectly related to observable phenomena. On the other hand, complementarity does not require us to treat models merely as useful fictions, or to accept a positivist interpretation. Complementarity when understood in this way is not inconsistent with critical realism.

3. NUMINOUS AND MYSTICAL EXPERIENCE

Within physics complementary models are used in the domain of the unobservably small, whose characteristics seem to be radically unlike those of everyday objects; the electron cannot be adequately visualized or consistently described by familiar analogies. Perhaps within religion also there are inherent limitations in the applicability of visualizable models and familiar analogies. We shall see whether personal and impersonal models of Ultimate Reality may be thought of as complementary representations. In accordance with the principle that we should start from the experiential basis of religion, we must consider first the fundamental types of religious experience which give rise to these two broad types of models.

There are two common types of religious experience which Ninian Smart has traced among world religions: numinous encounter (associated with worship) and mystical union (associated with meditation).[13] *Numinous encounter* received its classic description in Rudolf Otto's *The Idea of the Holy*. Its characteristics include a sense of awe and reverence, mystery and wonder, holiness and sacredness, fascination and dread. Typical examples are the vision of Isaiah in the temple, the call of Paul or Muhammad, or the theophany of Krishna in which Arjuna is struck dumb in amazement. Numinous experience is often accompanied by moral demand and a response of humility. It is institutionalized as worship, and as ritual ascribing value to the object of worship and expressing the inferiority of the worshipper (often symbolized by bowing down).

Smart asserts that numinous experience is usually interpreted by *personal models* of God. The worshipper thinks of God as distinct and separate from himself. The overwhelming character of the experience suggests an exalted view of the divine. The 'distance' between man and God, acknowledged in self-abasement, leads to an emphasis on the 'otherness' and transcendence of God (rather than to divine immanence as in the mystical tradition). The sense of being grasped and laid hold of, the unexpectedness and confrontation, and the conviction that one's response is evoked, all seem to point to an activity independent of man's own control, a divine rather than human initiative. Winston King, after describing the ritual-communal component of religion which expresses 'the gap between worshipping man and the worshipped Ultimate', concludes: 'We have here a root of personalistic theism, whatever may be the doctrine of the given tradition. For the ritualized forms of relationship tend to be those of personalized worship: sacrifice and petitionary prayer to a deity who will hear and heed.'[14]

The second type of experience, *mystical union*, also seems to have common characteristics, or at least 'family resemblances', in cultures which had almost no historical interaction. W. T. Stace has documented such recurrent traits as unitary consciousness and intense joy.[15] In some cases the unity is found in the world, the 'one' in the multiplicity of objects, as in nature mysticism. In other cases, the world is left behind on the inward route of contemplative discipline; undifferentiated unity is found in the depth of one's own soul. Despite such variations, there is considerable agreement in these descriptions. The Christian mystic can recognize the Hindu mystic's experience as similar to his own. Here the typical expression is meditation and contemplation rather than worship or ritual. Discipline, and sometimes asceticism, leads to peace, serenity and bliss. Sacrament and scripture are left behind in enlightenment, immediacy of knowledge, realization of unity, and liberation from the illusion of separation. In identity with the One beyond time and space, all differences are obliterated. All dichotomies (human-divine, subject-object, time-eternity, evil-good) are transcended.

The mystic is cautious in the use of models; he is likely to stress the ineffability of the experience. He may start from the *via negativa*, the assertion of what the divine is not; Brahman, says the Hindu, is *neti, neti* (not this, not this). But he usually does not stop there. 'The mystic must be silent: but he cannot be: he must speak.'[16] The images and models he does use are sometimes *personal*. He may speak of ultimate reality as a Self identical in essence with the individual self, or as the World Soul with which one's own soul is merged. Atman, man's true self, is Brahman, the divine found within; 'That art thou.' But mystical experience has more often been associated with *impersonal* images. The self is absorbed in the pantheistic All, the impersonal Absolute, the divine Ground. The distinction between subject and object is overcome in an all-embracing unity beyond all personal forms. The self loses its individuality 'as a raindrop loses its separate identity in the ocean'.[17]

Ninian Smart has shown that although Western religious traditions have been predominantly numinous and Eastern traditions predominantly mystical, all the major world religions have in fact included *both types of experience*.[18] Early Israel gave priority to the numinous; biblical literature portrays the overwhelming sense of encounter, the prophetic experience of the holy as personal, the acknowledgment of the gulf between the worshipper and the object of worship. But in later Judaism and Christianity there are many typically mystical writings. Islam in its early history was also strongly numinous, but later developed its own versions of mysticism, especially in Sufi literature. On the other hand, early Buddhism was predominantly mystical, following the meditative path, but Mahayana Buddhism includes the numinous strand in the worship of the heavenly Buddhas and Bodhisatvas. Evidence of both strands is present in all the major religious traditions. We shall explore them as a possible case of complementarity.

Although religious experience as described by Rudolf Otto is predominantly numinous, it includes a component which when more fully developed seems to lead towards mysticism. Otto spoke of the *mysterium tremendum et fascinans*, the mystery which evokes fear and awe, and yet also attracts and fascinates. Otto himself correlated this polarity with the tension between divine wrath and divine love, which is undoubtedly a characteristic form of interpretation in the West. But a more universal typology might correlate the *tremendum* pole with the prophet's feeling of the unapproachability of God, the radical discontinuity of Creator and creation, and the response of humility and prostration; man must keep his proper distance, of which any violation is *tabu*. The *fascinans* pole, on the other hand, resembles the mystic's feeling of the nearness of the divine, the continuity of all things, the participation of man in the ultimate identity. The polarity of withdrawal and approach, or distance and identity, seems to be present within the experience of the sacred, though for different individuals and traditions one aspect or the other may be more prominent. After discussing the prophetic and mystic traditions rooted in these two aspects of the experience of the sacred, Conrad Hyers concludes:

If pressed to their logical conclusions on the basis of their respective premises they become mutually exclusive visions which can only meet in tragic contradiction. Nevertheless, inasmuch as each articulated one side of a basic religious polarity, they are necessarily complementary visions . . . the solution to such historical oppositions and antagonisms is, therefore, a dialectical one – not in the Hegelian or Marxian sense of dialectic, but through a dialectic which acknowledges both sides of those paradoxes intrinsic to the religious situation. Such a dialectic is not strictly a synthesis, and certainly not an eclectic juxtaposition of elements; it is the recognition and realization of the implications of a fundamental duality in the presentation of and response to the sacred.[19]

Winston King has discussed the universal polarity of personal and impersonal symbols:

By and large the Eastern religions can be distinguished from Western religions specifically by their emphasis upon the impersonality of the ultimate Object of religious devotion. The terms used for ultimate realities in the East – Brahman, Nirvana, Tao, Heaven, and Kami – are almost entirely non-personal in connotation and experience. In the East, the personal form of existence and individual consciousness are looked upon as inferior and limited; they exist at a level of being and experience that does not accurately describe the truly Ultimate Reality.[20]

But King also points out that personal symbols of relation and impersonal symbols of identification co-exist in all the major traditions:

We will see how mingled the relational-personal and the identificatory-impersonal quality of symbols actually is in both East and West religious traditions. In anticipation: the non-God of the East often achieves personalistic forms and is so worshipped; and the God of the West has been more than once conceived of as impersonal reality.[21]

As an example, we shall consider the presence of both types of religious experience, and the corresponding interpretive models, in Hinduism. The *numinous* type recurs throughout the Bhagavadgita. The *bhakti* tradition has followed the path of devotion, the way to God through worship, loving adoration, and reliance on divine grace. To his devotees, Vishnu was the one God, the Supreme Person beyond the imperishable Brahman. For Ramanuja, the personal God was the Supreme Lord, worthy of dedicated worship, of whom the impersonal is only one manifestation. This approach is predominant in daily life and practice in India today. But the *mystical* approach is also prominent in the history of Hinduism. In Sankara's monism, there is one supreme Brahman, the Absolute without attributes. In the higher state of liberation through meditation, there is no 'other' to worship; the representation of God as Creator (Isvara) is merely a useful way of portraying the divine for the ordinary worshipper. Similarly, Vedanta Hinduism speaks of two levels of truth: the highest truth of One Ultimate Reality, known in contemplation, and a lower level in which Brahman can be viewed as personal creator and focus of worship.

A modern interpreter, S. Radhakrishnan, comments on the tolerance of Hinduism in allowing both *personal* and *impersonal* representations of the divine. They are, he says, two sides of the same reality, not incompatible claims or merely different human viewpoints:

> Western forms of religion are inclined to hold that one definition is final and absolute and others are false. In India, each definition represents a *darsana* or viewpoint. There are many different ways of viewing one experience. The different *darsanas* are different viewpoints which are not necessarily incompatible. They are pointers on the way to spiritual realization.[22]

Radhakrishnan holds that we can apply personal terms since the personal is the highest category we know in finite experience. Yet personal terms 'do not tell us about God in himself' but only what he is to us', but also as he 'expresses himself in a personal mode'. It appears that Radhakrishnan's view is finally monistic; the mystic's awareness of his spiritual identity with the suprapersonal Absolute is a higher goal than the worship of a personal God.

Vedanta Hinduism allows a place for theism, but tends to see it as a lower stage of spiritual development. The mystical strand is given priority over the worship of the personal, holy divinity. At the highest level of truth, the personal in both man and God is swallowed up in the impersonal Absolute. Moreover, the impersonality of the cosmic order in Hindu thought is reinforced by the idea of *karma* as an impersonal moral law concerning the inexorable consequences of one's deeds. From its side, Christianity has made room for mysticism but has preserved the dominance of the theistic framework. It has been critical of the extremes of pantheistic interpretation. It has found unacceptable any total identity which obliterates the gap between man and God, as in Meister Eckhart's statement: 'If I am to know God directly, I must become completely He and He I, so that this He and this I become and are one I.'[23] As analogy for the union of man and God, Christian mystics invoke the interpersonal unity of marriage more often than the impersonal merging of a drop in the ocean. Worship, rather than meditation, remains the basic Christian experience.

This relative priority of personal or impersonal models has far-reaching implications. Only with a personal God can there be divine initiative and freedom rather than cosmic necessity. Divine initiative, together with the ontological and epistemological distance assumed between man and God, is a correlate of the ideas of historical revelation, grace and redemption; the gulf can only be bridged from the side of the divine. Belief in a purposeful creator active in history has led to the conviction that the historical process is directional rather than cyclical. Again, Western traditions have given greater stress to human individuality (which in extreme forms becomes an anti-social individualism). Belief in the worth of the individual is in part based on an understanding of the value of persons to God. Man's freedom can of course be jeopardized as much by an omnipotent God as by a pantheistic determinism, but the West has usually viewed the self as an active agent. It has found a larger place for ethical activism, whereas the oriental quest for inner peace has more often led to quietism – though one can only admire the compassion and sensitivity of many of its saints and holy men. These relationships are of course very complex. They are mentioned here only as a reminder that any model functions in *a total network* of ideas and attitudes which form an interrelated and organic whole.

These differences between integral religious traditions – Hinduism and Christianity, for example – are so great that they can best be understood as the product of *different paradigms*. In the following three chapters I will analyse a paradigm as 'a tradition embodied in historical exemplars' and show how it dominates the patterns of life and thought of a scientific or a religious community. Thus I would propose that we should *not* refer to the Hindu Brahman and the Christian God as *complementary models* (if some analogy with quantum physics is thereby implied), since they are not used in the same paradigm community. However, the use of personal and impersonal models *within* the Hindu tradition, or *within* the Christian tradition, does seem to present some interesting parallels with complementarity in physics, which we must now examine further.

4. PERSONAL AND IMPERSONAL MODELS

Consider first the suggestion that two different personal models within a given tradition might be thought of as complementary. William Austin has developed Bohr's proposal mentioned earlier that the idea of complementarity may be applied to divine *love* and divine *justice* in biblical thought. After describing in some detail the principle of complementarity in physics, Austin suggests that images of God as Father and as Judge are complementary models used to interpret individual and corporate experience.[24] The prophet Amos, he points out, interpreted events in Israel's history primarily in terms of God's judgment, while Hosea understood events in terms of God's forgiveness. One possible explanation would be that these different models were used in different historical circumstances, just as there are 'different experimental situations' in physics. But it appears that they actually faced very similar historical situations, and both prophets made some use of both models. Even for Amos there was hope of forgiveness, at least for a remnant; and for Hosea, Israel was judged by the very love which would not abandon her. Here is a kind of mutual limitation, Austin proposes, in which the presence of one model prevents the exclusive development of the other. The models are taken in interaction rather than in total independence, and there is a tension between them as there is in quantum physics.

I suggest, however, that in this case a *compromise model* can be introduced. In human life, a loving father must remember the demands of justice, or else concern for his child becomes sentimentality. And a judge must have some scope for mercy, or else justice will become legalistic retribution. So the models of God as Father and as Judge can to some extent be merged, or perhaps included in a wider image – an ideal King, for example, who is both loving and just to his subjects. Moreover the guiding theme of the covenant provides a historical framework within which both love and justice have a place, even though in any particular situation their demands appear to be opposed. I do not see here quite the kind of mutual exclusiveness that exists between particles and waves, which prevents the development of a single compromise model in quantum physics.

A case which seems more analogous to complementarity in physics is Paul Tillich's use of *personal and impersonal symbols*, to which the remainder of this chapter is devoted. He acknowledges the importance of personalistic imagery in the biblical tradition. The Holy is known in the divine-human encounter, the person-to-person relation of mutual freedom, reciprocity and individuality. In guilt, forgiveness and faith, man responds to a God understood as a separate being who acts to save. But Tillich also frequently uses the impersonal symbols associated with mysticism. He presents 'individuation and participation' as one of the basic polarities which characterize all existence. Whereas I-Thou encounter symbolizes the individuation of man and God, the mystic's experience of unity points to participation in the divine. 'Individuation', taken alone, makes God and man separate beings under the sway of the subject-object distinction, but 'participation' alone leads to the loss of self-hood and freedom.[25]

Tillich finds evidence of the *personal-impersonal* polarity throughout biblical thought. If the Word of God is personal address to man, it is also the *Logos*, the rational structure of the cosmos, the universal creative power. If revelation is God manifest in unique historical events, it is also the divine self-manifestation in the depth of all events. If prayer is man's personal address to God, it is also surrender to that which is working in us, nearer than we are to ourselves. If love is reconciliation overcoming estrangement between personal beings, it is also the reunion of that which was separated, the recovery of a fundamental identity.[26]

Theistic *supernaturalism*, says Tillich, pictures God as a being, separate from all other beings. It portrays him by merely extending the categories of finitude – spatially, as above the world; temporally, as before the world; and causally, as a cause among other causes. But pantheistic *naturalism* makes God only a power within the world, ignoring 'the decisive element in the experience of the holy, namely the distance between finite man, on the one hand, and the holy in its numerous manifestations, on the other'. Pantheism also neglects the mutual freedom of man and God, the freedom of the created 'to turn away from its essential unity with its creative ground'.[27]

For Tillich, God is not *a* being, but *being-itself*. Some critics have assumed that 'being' is a lifeless, static, impersonal concept. But Tillich stresses the active power of being overcoming non-being, the power of life resisting the threat of death. God is the creative ground of being, the transcendent source of vitality and dynamics as well as of form and structure. God is not *a* person, for to Tillich an individual personal centre or self implies a radical separateness from everything else. But God is the ground of self-transcendence and personhood which is actualized in finite persons:

'Personal God' does not mean that God is *a* person. It means that God is the ground of everything personal and that he carries within himself the ontological power of personality. . . . Ordinary theism has made God a heavenly, completely perfect person who resides above the world and mankind. The protest of atheism against such a highest person is correct. There is no evidence for his existence, nor is he a matter of ultimate concern. God is not God without universal participation.[28]

Elsewhere Tillich writes:

This means that *being* and *person* are not contradictory concepts. Being includes personal being; it does not deny it. The ground of being is the ground of personal being, not its negation. . . . Religiously speaking, this means that our encounter with the God who is a person includes the encounter with the God who is the ground of everything personal and as such not *a* person. Religious experience, particularly as expressed in the great religions, exhibits a deep feeling for the tension between the personal and the nonpersonal element in the encounter between God and man. The Old as well as the New Testament has the astonishing power to speak of the divine in such a way that the I-thou character of the relation never darkens the transpersonal power and mystery of the divine, and vice versa.[29]

In the basic polarities of existence – individuation and participation, dynamics and form, freedom and destiny – the first term of each pair is more 'personal'. But both terms in each polarity must be included in the characterization of the divine life.

Any aspect of being can be a *symbol* of God since all being participates in being-itself. Religious symbols, says Tillich, participate in the reality they represent and thus point beyond themselves. They combine the concreteness of the specific events or objects from which they are drawn with the ultimacy of the ground which they symbolize. They are affirmed as symbols but denied as literal predications, for the categories of finitude cannot be applied literally to God. Use of a religious symbol demands self-criticism and awareness of its limitations. Nothing finite deserves worship; to elevate the symbol itself to ultimacy is idolatry. Literal language is also unable to express the existential involvement which is a precondition of apprehension of the divine. The use of a symbol, personal or impersonal, requires a dialectic of affirmation and negation.

Tillich suggests several *criteria* for evaluating religious symbols, in addition to this capacity for self-negation.[30] A symbol of the ultimate must transcend the subject-object division, for the characteristics of being-itself are equally present in human life and beyond it; the symbol must express the basic unity of all things, of which man is aware in the depths of his own being. Further, a symbol can be judged by its integrating or disintegrating power in practice. A symbol of the true ultimate will unify men as individuals and as communities rather than dividing them. Its effects will be creative rather than destructive and it will vindicate its promises of human fulfilment. A final criterion is the adequacy of the symbol to religious experience – its authenticity in expressing the state of a person grasped by an ultimate concern and in representing that which concerns him ultimately. Thus Tillich's theory of symbols stresses their religious use in expressing and evoking experience, and their role as vehicles of commitment and devotion.

Do personal or impersonal symbols predominate in Tillich's theology? To answer this, we must distinguish three sources of his theology whose influence varies among his diverse writings. First, there is the *experiential* basis of his thought. Here there is much in common with the impersonal features of the mystical tradition. In the heritage of the Neo-Platonic mystics, Jacob Boehme, and German mysticism, Tillich frequently talks about immediate awareness, the union of knower and known, the intuition of identity, and participation in a unity beyond the subject-object division. Man is grasped by the holy, the unconditional, the sacred. Tillich defines faith not as person-to-person trust but as 'ultimate concern', unconditional demand, the final ground of a person's values and the justification for his decisions. Whatever its object, ultimate concern is a total perspective involving the whole person and requiring his unreserved allegiance.

Tillich holds that theology must start from the 'questions' implied in human existence and the 'answers' experienced in human life in response to revelatory events. One such experience is *courage* overcoming the anxiety of finitude, temporality and meaninglessness. In accepting ourselves as accepted we participate in the self-affirmation of being-itself; we seek the sustaining power which undergirds and supports our courage to be in the face of the threat of non-being. Another basic experience is *reconciliation* overcoming separation and estrangement. The redemptive power of love is known in human life. Grace and redemption are not theological abstractions but experienced realities in which divisions within man, and between man and his neighbour, are healed. Salvation is literally 'being made whole' by the healing forces at work in the world. God is the structure of reality and the power of being which brings about these transformations of human existence, which can be described in personal terms as response to love and forgiveness and in ontological terms as the reunion of the separated.

In the second source of Tillich's theology, *the biblical tradition*, personalistic symbols are more strongly represented. His description of reconciliation is of course indebted to biblical formulations, but his presentation of Christ as the New Being in whom is manifest the power of love brings out more fully the importance of personal symbols. Tillich acknowledges that the divine is manifest to particular communities in the concreteness of revelatory events and persons. For the Christian community, the cross is the supreme symbol, for in his self-sacrifice Christ pointed beyond himself and surrendered the particular to the ultimate; the cross was the manifestation of God's participation in man's existence, universally present but not universally recognized.[31] Tillich's own background in the Lutheran Church and his sensitivity to Luther's experience of guilt, forgiveness, personal faith and divine grace, are reflected at many points in his writings, especially in his sermons.[32]

But the third source of Tillich's thought, the tradition of *German idealist philosophy*, gives greater emphasis to impersonal conceptions and is more evident in his systematic discussion of the doctrine of God.[33] He does not accept Hegel's vision of participation in the all-inclusive Absolute in which all differences are overcome in harmonious synthesis. Rather, with Schelling, he conceives of the finite as both participating in and estranged from the infinite. Revelation must come to man, and yet it comes not as something alien and foreign. Estrangement is fragmentarily overcome by love, not totally resolved by rational synthesis. Yet for Tillich, man's essential unity with the infinite is never destroyed by man's actual estrangement. The basic identity of thought and being, the unity of subject and object, and the possibility of immediate awareness by participation, which are assumptions of Western idealism from Plato to Hegel, are all fundamental to Tillich's viewpoint. The ontological structures of the world, the unity underlying polarity, are the clues to understanding God. The differentiation of separate selves is not a reflection of the goodness of creation but a source of ambiguity and division. When man discovers God he finds something identical with himself, not a stranger or an inference at the end of an argument.[34]

It seems to me, then, that even though Tillich's theory of symbols dwells on religious uses, and his theological method starts from existential questions, his formal discussion of God is more strongly indebted to idealist philosophy than to either religious experience or the biblical tradition. In his other writings, models of God serve mainly religious functions, but in his systematic doctrine of God models serve mainly metaphysical functions and are greatly influenced by a philosophical ontology in which impersonal categories predominate. God may be transpersonal (beyond the distinction between personal and impersonal), but our models must use analogies from the life with which we are familiar, and for Tillich it is the impersonal structures which are emphasized. In Chapter 8 below I will suggest that process metaphysics is more congenial to the personalistic models characteristic of biblical thought, while including impersonal features of the cosmic evolutionary process.

In concluding this chapter we must ask whether personal and impersonal models in such a theology as Tillich's could be considered *complementary*. I can see a certain parallel with the situation in atomic physics: the use of two models which cannot be combined, along with recognition of the limitations of all models and the inadequacy of literalism. Is there a greater contrast between personal and impersonal models than between waves and particles? Perhaps there are fewer common properties in the first polarity than in the second, but we should not minimize the divergence in conceptualities between waves and particles. (One might even speculate that particles represent 'individuation' in separate units, whereas waves represent a kind of 'participation' in a more inclusive field.) The main parallel is simply that in both situations two contrasting types of models are used.

There are also features of complementarity in atomic physics which are absent from theology. In atomic physics there is a unifying mathematical formalism which allows at least probabilistic prediction of particular observations. There is consistency at the level of *theory*, though not at the level of *models*. Theory specifies what is essential in the models by indicating the positive and negative analogies. In theology, doctrinal schemes provide some conceptual unity in the quest for coherence, and they serve a function not unlike that of theories. But their relation to experience is more ambiguous, and no one would claim for them any kind of predictive power on even a probabilistic basis. We will explore theory and observation in science and religion in the next two chapters, before returning to models in Chapter 8.

6

Paradigms in Science

———

WE MUST NOW carry further our analysis of the structure of science. Scientific models lead to theories which can be tested against observations. We must examine this process of assessment in science, and then compare it with the process of assessment in religion in the succeeding chapters.

Among criteria for assessing scientific theories are simplicity, coherence and agreement with experimental evidence. *Simplicity* is sought both as a practical advantage and as an intellectual ideal. This includes not only simplicity of mathematical form, conceptual simplicity, and a minimum of independent assumptions, but also an aesthetic element. It is not uncommon to hear scientists refer to the beauty or elegance or symmetry of a theory. *Coherence* with other accepted theories is also sought. The scientist aims at the comprehensive unification of separate laws, the systematic interrelation of theories, the portrayal of underlying similarities in apparently diverse phenomena. But the most important criterion is the number and variety of *supporting experimental observations*. A theory is valued if it accurately accounts for known observations and yields precise predictions of future measurements. The scientist is particularly impressed if it explains a variety of types of phenomena and, above all, if it leads to the discovery of novel phenomena not previously anticipated.

The empiricist accounts of science which were prevalent in the 1950's emphasized agreement with experiment as the main criterion for judging between rival theories. They defended the *objectivity* of science through three claims. (1) Science starts from publicly observable data which can be described in a pure observation-language independent of any theoretical assumptions. (2) Theories can then be verified or falsified by comparison with this fixed experimental data. (3) The choice between rival theories is thus rational, objective, and in accordance with specifiable criteria.

These ideas came under increasing attack in the late 1950's and early 1960's, and three counter-claims were advanced. (1) *All data are theory-laden*; there is no neutral observation-language. (2) *Theories are not verified or falsified*; when data conflict with an accepted theory, they are usually set to one side as anomalies, or else auxiliary assumptions are modified. (3) *There are no criteria for choice between rival theories* of great generality, for the criteria are themselves theory-dependent.

The attack on empiricism was carried a step further in Thomas Kuhn's *The Structure of Scientific Revolutions* (1962). Kuhn held that the thought and action of a scientific community are dominated by its *paradigms*, defined as 'standard examples of scientific work which embody a set of conceptual, methodological and metaphysical assumptions'. He maintained that observational data and criteria for assessing theories are paradigm-dependent. Paradigms are therefore 'incommensurable'. A shift of paradigms during a scientific revolution is not a matter of logical argument but of 'conversion'. Kuhn, according to his critics, portrayed scientific choice as irrational, subjective, and relative to particular scientific communities.

However, in the Postscript to the second edition (1970) of his book and in other recent essays, Kuhn has clarified and in some respects altered his earlier position; he now gives greater attention to the control of theory by experiment and the role of criteria independent of particular paradigms. On the other hand, some of the empiricists have qualified their assertions to take Kuhn's viewpoint into account. There is thus some evidence of convergence from the former 'objective' and 'subjective' extremes towards a middle position on each of the three points of disagreement. We will examine them in turn; it will be suggested later that each has significant implications for our understanding of religion.

1. THE INFLUENCE OF THEORY ON OBSERVATION

We shall first look briefly at new views of the relation of theory and observation. During the 1930's and 1940's there was wide acceptance of the positivist contention that science starts from indubitable data which can be described in a *neutral observation-language* independent of all theories. It was held that all theoretical terms must be translatable into pure observational terms by means of operational definitions. What does the scientist do? He collects objective data and then forms inductive generalizations, according to the early positivists. Here was an emphasis on *observation* and its independence from theory.

It is well known that this positivist position was criticized by both scientists and philosophers. For one thing, it left out the place of creative imagination in the formation of theories. A theory is not given to us ready-made by the data, or by inferences from the data; it is a mental construct, a human invention. Often an important advance has come, not from new data, but from a new way of looking at old data. Furthermore, a theoretical term cannot be translated into equivalent observation terms, for it may be related to new types of observation which cannot be foreseen or specified. Theoretical entities are often only very indirectly related to observations – especially in modern physics.

Now the versions of empiricism which were current in the 1950's took these criticisms into account. The importance of theoretical terms and non-observable entities in science was recognized. But it was still assumed that there are *fixed observational data* free from any theoretical interpretation. Nagel, Hempel, Braithwaite, Popper, and others[1] pictured two distinct levels in science: an unproblematic lower level of unchanging, objective data, describable in a pure observation language on which all observers can agree; and a separate upper level of theoretical constructs, acknowledged as products of man's creative imagination. In this scheme, the experimental data provide a neutral and impartial court of appeal for testing predictions deduced from alternative theories. The firm foundations of the scientific edifice are the solid data common to all observers. Here was an emphasis on both *theory* and *observation*, with a sharp distinction between them.

But during the 1960's even these modified versions of empiricism came under attack. Kuhn, Hanson, Polanyi, Feyerabend, Toulmin and others[2] concluded from their work in the history of science that the philosophers and logicians who set forth the empiricist position had not looked carefully enough at the real work of scientists. There are *no bare uninterpreted data*. Expectations and conceptual commitments influence perceptions, both in everyday life and in science. Man supplies the categories of interpretation, right from the start. The very language in which observations are reported is influenced by prior theories. The predicates we use in describing the world and the categories with which we classify events depend on the kinds of regularities we anticipate. The presuppositions which the scientist brings to his enquiry are reflected in the way he formulates a problem, the kind of apparatus he builds, and the type of variable he considers important. Here the emphasis is on *theory* and the way it permeates observation.

In N. R. Hanson's oft-quoted words, '*All data are theory-laden.*' The procedures of measurement and the interpretation of the resulting numerical values depend on implicit theoretical assumptions. Most of the time, of course, scientists work within a framework of thought which they have inherited. Most scientists in their day-to-day work presuppose the concepts and background theories of their day; in testing theories of limited scope they can therefore obtain unambiguous data which can be described in a commonly accepted observation-language. But, says Feyerabend, when the background theory itself is at issue, when the fundamental assumptions and basic concepts are under attack, then the dependence of measurement on theoretical assumptions is crucial. 'Every theory has its own observation language.' Consequently, comprehensive theories are 'incommensurable'.[3]

Feyerabend maintains that in the switch from Newtonian physics to relativity there was *a change in the meaning* of all the basic terms. Time, length, mass, velocity, even the notion of simultaneity, were redefined in the new system. In classical physics, mass was an inherent and unchanging property of a body. In relativity, however, mass is a property of the relationship between a body and a frame of reference, i.e., the mass of an object increases with an increase in its velocity relative to the observer. The equivalence of mass and energy – totally unexpected by the Newtonian – follows directly. Similarly, the distance and the time interval between two given events will be different for observers in different frames of reference, i.e., moving with respect to each other. Of course the Newtonian equations for the motion of an object can all be obtained from Einstein's equations as limiting cases for velocities which are small compared to the velocity of light. But even identical formulas are not equivalent if their terms have different meanings, according to Feyerabend.[4]

In response to this thesis that theories are incommensurable, several recent authors have acknowledged that all data are indeed theory-laden, but have insisted that there is a very wide variation in the degree to which *any given observation* is dependent on *any given theory*. In most experiments the data are not affected by the differences between the immediate hypotheses being compared; therefore the observations do exert some control over the choice of hypothesis. Moreover, expectations influence but do not completely determine what we see; unexpected events may make us revise our expectations. Israel Scheffler, replying to Feyerabend, writes:

> Our expectations strongly structure what we see, but do not wholly eliminate unexpected sights . . . Our categorizations and expectations guide by orienting us selectively towards the future; they set us, in particular, to perceive in certain ways and not in others. Yet they do not blind us to the unforeseen.[5]

When two theories conflict, their protagonists can withdraw, not to a supposedly pure observation language, but to an observation language whose theoretical assumptions are not immediately at issue. There will usually be enough overlap between the assumptions of the two parties that a *common core of observations-statements* can be accepted by both – even, I would argue, in a change as far-reaching as that from classical physics to relativity. Proponents of these two theories could agree as to how to measure the observed angle between two stars, even though they disagreed concerning the geometry of space. When the two theories yielded different views of the simultaneity of distant events, both parties could retreat to observations on which they concurred, namely the simultaneity of two signals reaching a single point. From the equivalence of mass and energy in relativity theory, together with theories about the fission of heavy nuclei, it was predicted that if a certain mass of uranium was brought together, an explosion would occur; surely all observers in the New Mexico desert on that day in 1943 could agree as to whether an explosion occurred.

But note that the shared *observational core*, against which competing theories may be tested, is not in general free from *theoretical interpretation*. The overlapping assumptions common to two theories will not be the same in all periods of history; they carry no guarantee of infallibility. Moreover, the categories of classification employed in an observational description may themselves need to be revised in the light of subsequent developments in the theory. Scheffler acknowledges that though observation exerts a control over theory, any given observation statement may find itself overridden in the end and subject to modification (here he significantly departs from earlier empiricist assumptions). Theory is revisable in the light of observation, but observation may also sometimes need to be reconsidered in the light of theory.[6]

Thus the line between *observation* and *theory* is not sharp or fixed. The decision to look on a given statement as primarily theoretical or primarily observational is relative, pragmatic, and context-dependent, as Mary Hesse contends.[7] The emphasis may shift with the advance of science and the immediate purposes of enquiry. The 'standard observables' of one period will differ from those of another. What one treats as basic and uninterpreted will also vary according to the theory one is testing. Those descriptions which one considers more stable and more directly accessible will be taken as data, but that judgment will itself reflect theoretical assumptions. Hopefully this kind of account can represent both the more observational and the more theoretical poles of science and the interaction between them. It accepts the idea that there is no pure observation language, but it does not accept the claim that theories are incommensurable.

2. ON THE FALSIFIABILITY OF THEORIES

Let us look next at the debate as to whether or not theories can be verified or falsified. To the positivists, *verification* had seemed a clear-cut and straight-forward process. It was assumed that theories are verified by their agreement with experimental data. Knowledge, it was said, consists of proven propositions established by the hard facts. The famous 'Verification Principle' went on to assert that, apart from formal definitions, the only meaningful statements are empirical propositions verifiable by sense-experience. To rehearse the inadequacies of positivism now would be whipping a dead horse, but some of the reasons for the rejection of the idea of verification in science should be mentioned.

No scientific theory can be *verified*. One cannot prove that a theory is true by showing that conclusions deduced from it agree with experiment, since (1) future experiments may conflict with the theory, and (2) another theory may be equally compatible with present evidence. From a finite set of particular observations one cannot derive a universal generalization with certainty (the much debated logic of induction can provide no inferential grounds for making assertions about *all* cases when only a particular group of cases has been examined). In science, all theoretical formulations are tentative and subject to revision. Newtonian physics, one of the most extensively developed and experimentally supported theoretical systems in the history of science, was overthrown by relativity; we have seen that Einstein challenged almost all of Newton's basic concepts. No theory today is immune to modification or replacement.

Cannot theories at least be *falsified*, then? Even if many instances of agreement with experiment do not prove that a theory is true, it would seem that even a single counterinstance of data which disagrees with theory should conclusively prove it false. Karl Popper, acknowledging that scientific theories are never verifiable, contended that they must be in principle *falsifiable*. Science advances by bold conjectures and stern attempts to refute them. Popper dwelt on the importance of 'crucial experiments' through which an hypothesis is definitively eliminated. Intellectual honesty, he said, requires the scientist to specify in advance experiments whose results could disprove his theory. Statements which are in principle unfalsifiable have no place in science.[8]

But Popper's view has in turn received considerable criticism. Discordant data *do not always falsify* a theory. One can never test an individual hypothesis conclusively in a 'crucial experiment'; for if a deduction is not confirmed experimentally, one cannot be sure which one, from among the many assumptions on which the deduction was based, was in error. A network of theories and observations is always tested together. Any particular hypothesis can be maintained by rejecting or adjusting other auxiliary hypotheses.[9] As Quine puts it, theories form a field which is only loosely tied to the data at its boundaries:

> The total field is so under-determined by its boundary condition, experience, that there is much latitude of choice as to what statements to re-evaluate in the light of a single contrary experience. No particular experiences are lined up with any particular statements in the interior of the field, except indirectly through considerations of equilibrium affecting the field as a whole . . . Any statement can be held true, come what may, if we make drastic enough adjustments elsewhere in the system.[10]

In practice the scientist works within the framework of accepted assumptions, and throws all the doubt on one new hypothesis at a time; but it might be just the accepted assumptions which should be questioned.

Many authors have criticized the idea of 'crucial experiments', but I want to comment particularly on the recent writings of Imre Lakatos because they show how far he has moved from Popper's position, even though he presents his own view as a modification of Popper's. In some cases of discrepancy between theory and data, he points out, it is the *implicit theoretical assumptions in the data* which have been challenged. The use of data presupposes theories about the operation of instruments and the interpretation of experimental procedures, any of which may be questioned. Lakatos writes that 'stubborn theoreticians frequently challenge experimental verdicts and have them reversed.' Newton, for example, told the Astronomer Royal, Flamsteed, to correct some astronomical data because it disagreed with theoretical predictions; several factors, including refraction of light by the atmosphere, were later proposed to justify the corrections.[11]

Auxiliary hypotheses may be introduced to remove a disagreement. A classic instance was the beta-decay of the nucleus, in which experimental data seemed clearly to violate the law of conservation of energy. Rather than abandon this law, physicists postulated an unobservable particle, the neutrino, to account for the discrepancy. Only at a considerably later point was there any independent evidence for the existence of the neutrino. Another case was Prout's theory that the atoms of all elements are composed of hydrogen atoms, which implied that the atomic weights of all elements should be whole numbers (integers). Experiments giving 35.5 as the atomic weight of chlorine seemed to refute his theory, but he insisted that the assumptions implicit in the techniques for purifying the gas must be erroneous. He was unable to support this auxiliary hypothesis. Yet one can see a partial vindication of his theory in the later discovery that samples separated by physical rather than chemical means into pure isotopes do indeed have atomic weights which are almost exactly integral multiples of the atomic weight of hydrogen.[12]

Whether or not a given procedure is considered a '*crucial experiment*' will vary with the changing theoretical context. At one point Fizeau's measurement of the velocity of light in water seemed a conclusive refutation of the corpuscular theory of light; but the latter returned, in a new form, in Einstein's theory of photons. Again, Michelson designed in 1881 a 'crucial experiment' whose results, he claimed, were a proof that the ether is dragged along with the earth, disproving the stationary ether theory. But Lorentz showed that the latter is not refuted if bodies change dimensions when moving (the Fitzgerald–Lorentz contraction). Later Einstein on other grounds developed the theory of relativity; only then did the Michelson–Morley experiment, performed twenty-five years earlier, appear as important evidence against all ether theories.

'Crucial experiments' are only recognizable by hindsight, relative to the historical development of a theoretical system. The term is honorific, bestowed long after the event by the victorious party. For, in Lakatos' words, a theory can lose several battles and yet come back to win the war, if its supporters do not give up too easily.[13]

Finally, a recurrent discrepancy may simply be set aside as an *unexplained anomaly*. Newton's theory of gravitation predicted that the apogee (most distant point) of the moon's elliptical orbit around the earth should move forward $1\frac{1}{2}°$ each revolution. Newton admitted in his *Principia* that the observed motion was twice that predicted. For sixty years this disagreement, which was far beyond the limits of experimental error, could not be accounted for, yet it was never taken to 'falsify' the theory. More recently, the advance of the perihelion of Mercury was treated as an anomaly for eighty-five years, and only after the advent of relativity theory was it taken as evidence against Newtonian mechanics. The history of science is replete with such anomalies which for varying periods have been left unexplained.[14]

It is worth noting that a theory of great generality is usually abandoned only in favour of an *alternative theory*, not just because of conflicting data. A theory which seems defective at a few points is better than none at all. In the absence of an alternative, one can usually doctor up the old theory with suitable amendments, though there may eventually be so many patches and *ad hoc* adjustments that in the interests of simplicity one starts looking for alternatives. In practice, then, discordant observations are important, but they do not have any absolute power to falsify a theory, especially a comprehensive one.

One of the points at which Lakatos differs most markedly from Popper, and most resembles Kuhn, is his defence of *commitment* to a 'research programme'. He urges that our attention be directed, not to individual hypotheses, nor even to theoretical networks at any one point in time, but to developing research programmes over a span of time – such as the Newtonian programme to treat the universe as a mechanical system, or Bohr's programme for the quantization of atomic systems. Lakatos' programmes, like Kuhn's paradigms, are not falsifiable in any direct way. For he holds that the 'hard core' of a programme (Newton's Laws, for instance) is by deliberate decision made *exempt from falsification* so that its positive possibilities can be explored; any adjustments to accommodate counter-instances are confined to non-essential secondary assumptions. 'This core is "irrefutable" by methodological decision of its protagonists; anomalies must lead to change only in the "protective" belt of auxiliary "observational" hypotheses and initial conditions.'[15] This decision is not a declaration that the programme is true; it is a methodological device, a useful strategy for systematically developing the 'positive heuristic' without too many distractions. It is a policy for determining which hypotheses are to be considered essential to the programme, to be retained as long as possible, and which hypotheses are non-essential, to be sacrificed when difficulties occur.

Lakatos defines a *research programme* as 'progressive' if in the long run it leads to the discovery of novel phenomena and previously unexpected facts as well as accounting for facts already known. A programme is 'degenerative' and should be abandoned when (1) it has stalled for long enough and (2) there are promising alternatives. In such a degenerative stage, there will usually be an accumulation of *ad hoc* modifications for which there is no independent evidence. There will be no growth, over a protracted period of time, in the corroborated empirical content of the hard-core theories. But Lakatos maintains that there are no clear-cut rules for judging when a period is protracted enough, or the novelty slight enough, or the alternatives promising enough, to warrant relinquishing a programme. Here Lakatos, like Kuhn, holds that only scientists themselves can decide, in particular historical contexts, whether to stick with a research programme or not. In the next chapter, such commitment to a programme will be compared to commitment in religion.

3. COMMITMENT TO PARADIGMS

Of the exponents of new views of the relation of theories and observations, Thomas Kuhn has been the most influential. One discussion of his ideas lists thirty-six reviews of *The Structure of Scientific Revolutions* in journals whose fields range from philosophy and science to psychology and sociology.[16] Many scientists feel at home in the volume because it gives frequent concrete examples from the history of science and seems to describe science as they know it. But others hold that he gives far too much prominence to subjective aspects of science. Workers in new research fields in the natural sciences, and in areas of the behavioural sciences where basic concepts and fundamental assumptions are in dispute, often find Kuhn's writing illuminating. I will summarize four themes of his book as it originally appeared, and then indicate some of the criticisms it has evoked and his subsequent reply to his critics. The debate reveals a new understanding of the nature of science which has far-reaching implications.

1. *Paradigms dominate normal science.* Kuhn maintains that every scientific community is dominated by a cluster of very broad conceptual and methodological presuppositions embodied in the 'standard examples' through which students learn the prevailing theories of the field. Because such examples also serve as norms of what constitutes good science, they transmit methodological and metaphysical assumptions along with key concepts. A paradigm, such as Newton's work in mechanics, implicitly defines for a given scientific community the types of question that may legitimately be asked, the types of explanation that are to be sought, and the types of solution that are acceptable. It moulds the scientist's assumptions as to what kinds of entity there are in the world (Newton was interested in matter in motion) and the methods of enquiry suitable for studying them. 'Some accepted examples of actual scientific practice – examples which include law, theory, application and instrumentation together – provide models from which spring particular coherent traditions of scientific research.'[17]

Normal science, says Kuhn, consists of work within the framework of a paradigm which defines a coherent research tradition. Scientific education is an induction into the habits of thought and activity presented by text books, and an initiation into the practice of established scientists. It leads to the acquisition of 'a strong network of commitments, conceptual, theoretical, instrumental, and methodological'. Paradigms illustrate ways of attacking a problem – for instance, by analysis in terms of masses and forces. Thereby they guide the direction of normal research, which is 'an attempt to force nature into the preformed and relatively inflexible boxes that the paradigm supplies'.[18] Like solving a puzzle or playing a game of chess, normal science seeks solutions within an accepted framework; the rules of the game are already established. A shared paradigm creates a scientific community – a professional grouping with common assumptions, interests, journals and channels of communication. This stress on the importance of the community suggests parallels in the role of the religious community which will be explored later.

2. *Scientific revolutions are paradigm shifts.* Kuhn holds that in normal research fundamental assumptions are not questioned. Anomalies are set to one side, or accommodated by *ad hoc* modifications. Ptolemaic astronomy went on adding planetary epicycles to remove discrepancies; defenders of the phlogiston theory were driven to postulate negative chemical weights in order to maintain their paradigm. But with a growing list of anomalies, a sense of crisis leads the scientific community to examine its assumptions and to search for alternatives. A new paradigm may then be proposed which challenges the dominant presuppositions.

Kuhn shows that when a major change of paradigm does occur it has such far-reaching effects that it amounts to a revolution. Paradigms are incompatible. A new paradigm replaces the old; it is not merely one more addition to a cumulative structure of ideas. A revolution from Aristotelian to Newtonian physics, for instance, or from Newtonian physics to relativity, is 'a transformation of the scientific imagination' in which old data are seen in entirely new ways. For a period, adherents of two different paradigms may be competing for the allegiance of their colleagues, and the choice is not unequivocally determined by the normal criteria of research. Kuhn writes:

Though each may hope to convert the other to his way of seeing his science and its problems, neither may hope to prove his case. The competition between paradigms is not the sort of battle that can be resolved by proofs . . . Before they can hope to communicate fully, one group or the other must experience the conversion that we have been calling a paradigm shift. Just because it is a transition between incommensurables, the transition between competing paradigms cannot be made a step at a time, forced by logic and neutral experience. Like a gestalt switch it must occur all at once or not at all.[19]

Scientists resist such revolutions because previous commitments have permeated all their thinking; a new paradigm prevails only when the older generation has been 'converted' to it, or has died off and been replaced by a new generation. As Kuhn portrays it, a paradigm shift is thus a highly subjective process. He claims that scientific revolutions, like political revolutions, do not employ the normal methods of change.

3. *Observations are paradigm-dependent.* Kuhn agrees with Feyerabend and Hanson that there is no neutral observation language. Paradigms determine the way a scientist sees the world. Galileo saw a swinging pendulum as an object with inertia, which almost repeats its oscillating motion; his predecessors, inheriting the Aristotelian interest in progress towards final ends, had seen a pendulum as a constrained falling object, which slowly attains its final state of rest. (Note the recurrence of the expression 'seeing as', whose use by Wittgenstein and Wisdom was mentioned earlier.) As with a gestalt switch, the same situation can be seen in differing ways. Scientists with rival paradigms may gather quite dissimilar sorts of data; the very features which are important for one may be incidental to the other. Rival paradigms, says Kuhn, solve different types of problems; they are, like Feyerabend's basic theories, 'incommensurable'.[20]

4. *Criteria are paradigm-dependent.* Competing paradigms offer differing judgments as to what sorts of solution are acceptable. There are no external standards on which to base a choice between paradigms, for standards are themselves products of paradigms. One can assess theories within the framework of a paradigm, but in a debate among paradigms there are no objective criteria. Paradigms cannot be falsified and are highly resistant to change. Adoption of a new paradigm is a 'conversion'. Each revolution, says Kuhn:

. . . necessitated the community's rejection of one time-honoured scientific theory in favour of another incompatible with it. Each produced a consequent shift in the problems available for scientific scrutiny and in the standards by which the profession determined what should count as an admissible problem or a legitimate problem-solution. And each transformed the scientific imagination in ways that we shall ultimately need to describe as a transformation of the world within which scientific work was done.[21]

Yet in one of his final chapters Kuhn does state that there are reasons, even 'hard-headed arguments', for the adoption of a new paradigm. Its proponents must try to show that it can solve the problems which led to the crisis of the old paradigm. They can sometimes point to quantitative precision or to the prediction of novel phenomena not previously suspected. But in the very early stages the enthusiasts for a new paradigm may have little empirical support to offer, while the traditionalists may have many solved problems to their credit, despite unresolved anomalies. And even at later stages there is seldom anything approaching a conclusive proof of the superiority of one paradigm over another.[22] This question of criteria for choice of paradigms is perhaps the most important issue in the controversy over Kuhn's book.

4. PARADIGMS RECONSIDERED

Since its first appearance, Kuhn's volume has provoked extensive discussion. He has had enthusiastic supporters and strenuous critics. Each of the four theses outlined above has been attacked:

1. *Criticisms of 'normal science'*. Kuhn's critics complain that his concept of paradigm is vague and ambiguous. Masterman lists twenty-one different senses of paradigm in the book. Kuhn's portrayal of the authoritarian character of normal science has also been challenged. Popper argues that in science there is continual criticism of fundamental assumptions; only beginning students or routine workers in applied science would uncritically accept dominant presuppositions. The scientist, he asserts, can challenge prevailing views whenever he wants to. 'If we try, we can break out of our framework at any time.' Feyerabend maintains that there is,

and should be, a multiplicity of basic alternatives present at all times, rather than the exclusive monopoly by one paradigm which Kuhn describes and defends. Normal science is more diverse and more self-critical than Kuhn recognizes.[23]

2. *Criticisms of 'scientific revolutions'*. Apart from the difficulty in identifying when a change is a 'revolution' and when it isn't, the sharp contrast between normal and revolutionary science has been questioned. S. E. Toulmin finds frequent small changes more typical of science – 'micro-revolutions' which do not fit either of Kuhn's two classifications. In addition, he alleges, the struggle of alternative views occurs not simply in rare crises but more or less continuously. There are many gradations between routine and extraordinary science, differences of degree rather than of kind. There is also more continuity across a revolution than Kuhn depicts; there may be changes in assumptions, instrumentation and data, but there are no total discontinuities.[24]

3. *Criticisms of 'the paradigm-dependence of observations'*. Even if a new paradigm directs attention to new problems and new variables, the old data need not be discarded and much of it may still be relevant. Dudley Shapere insists that under successive paradigms there are partly overlapping vocabularies; otherwise there could be no possibility of communication or public discussion. If two paradigms really were 'incommensurable', they could not be 'incompatible'; to be considered 'rivals' they must at least apply to a jointly identifiable phenomenon, describable in predicates shared by both protagonists. Moreover, though a paradigm determines which variables to study, it does not determine what the values of those variables will be. It may be resistant to falsification, but an accumulation of discordant data cannot be dismissed if empirical testing is to be maintained.[25]

4. *Criticisms of 'the paradigm-dependence of criteria'*. If observations as well as criteria are paradigm-dependent, there is no rational basis for choice among competing paradigms. Each paradigm determines its own criteria, so any argument for it is circular. The choice seems arbitrary and subjective, a matter of psychology and sociology more than of logic. Lakatos writes:

For Kuhn scientific change – from one 'paradigm' to another – is a mystical conversion which is not and cannot be governed by rules of reason and which falls totally within the realm of the (*social*) *psychology of discovery*. Scientific change is a kind of religious change . . . There are no rational standards for their comparison. Each paradigm contains its own standards. The crisis sweeps away not only the old theories and rules but also the standards which made us respect them. The new paradigm brings a totally new rationality. There are no super-paradigmatic standards. The change is a band wagon effect. Thus *in Kuhn's view scientific revolution is irrational, a matter of mob psychology*.[26]

It is on this point that Kuhn's critics are most vehement, accusing him of *relativism, subjectivism* and *irrationality*. Paradigm preference can be discussed only relative to a particular community. Watkins contrasts the dogmatism in Kuhn's 'closed societies' with the continuous criticism in Popper's 'open societies' and concludes: 'My suggestion is, then, that Kuhn sees the scientific community on the analogy of a religious community and sees science as the scientist's religion.'[27] Popper himself says: 'The Myth of the Framework is, in our time, the central bulwark of irrationalism. . . . In science, as distinct from theology, a critical comparison of the competing theories, of the competing frameworks, is always possible.'[28] Kuhn's portrayal of normal science as dominated by unchallenged dogmas, his failure to specify criteria for paradigm choice, and his talk of 'conversion' and 'persuasion' all seem to these critics to threaten the objectivity and rationality of the scientific enterprise.

In response to his critics, Kuhn has added a Postscript in the second edition of his book, and has written several essays, in which he clarifies his earlier views and at some points significantly modifies them. Since his final position does answer some of his critics' objections, his more recent treatment of each of the four themes presented above should be outlined:

1. *The diverse meanings of 'paradigm'*. Kuhn now tries to distinguish some of the various features of science which were formerly lumped together. Paradigms in their primary meaning are shared crucial examples, for which he suggests the term *exemplars*. One learns science by concrete examples of problem-solving, rather than by explicit rules. A formula, such as $f = ma$, is of little use until one learns how to approach a new situation so that it can be applied. One 'learns to see situations as like each other', and to recognize

similarities which have not been formalized. Kuhn holds that the extension of such similarities, embodied in exemplars, is important for normal research as well as for the science student.[29]

The more general 'constellation of group commitments' Kuhn now wants to call *the disciplinary matrix*. One component consists of widely held *values*, such as simplicity, consistency and predictive accuracy (these will be examined in connection with criteria below, since Kuhn acknowledges that they are widely shared among different scientific communities). Another component consists of metaphysical commitments transmitted by *particular models*:

> Re-writing the book now I would describe such commitments as beliefs in particular models, and I would expand the category models to include also the relatively heuristic variety: the electric circuit may be regarded as a steady-state hydrodynamic system; the molecules of a gas behave like tiny elastic billiard balls in random motion. Though the strength of group commitment varies, with non-trivial consequences, along the spectrum from heuristic to ontological models, all models have similar functions. Among other things they supply the group with preferred or permissible analogies and metaphors. By doing so they help to determine what will be accepted as an explanation and as a puzzle-solution; conversely, they assist in the determination of the roster of unsolved puzzles and in the evaluation of the importance of each.[30]

By introducing these distinctions, Kuhn has modified his earlier idea of the unity of a paradigm as a total coherent viewpoint, though it is not clear just how he thinks of the separate components of the disciplinary matrix as interacting with each other.

2. *The distinction between 'normal' and 'revolutionary' science*. Kuhn qualifies this distinction but still defends it. He now wants a 'scientific community' to be identified sociologically (e.g. by its patterns of inter-communication) before its shared paradigms are studied. Some 'communities' turn out to be quite small – as few as a hundred scientists. There can be considerable variation among competing 'schools of thought'. We are told that members of a community can disagree about some rather fundamental issues; nineteenth-century chemists did not all have to accept atomism as long as they all accepted the laws of combining proportions. Further, there can be 'small-scale revolutions' and 'micro-revolutions' (without a preceding crisis) affecting specialized subgroups

within a larger community. Nevertheless Kuhn still maintains that the most fruitful strategy of normal science is to develop and exploit the prevailing tradition, extending its scope and accuracy; the examination of assumptions and the search for alternatives, he holds, seldom occurs except during major crises.[31]

3. *The 'translation' of observations*. Kuhn has also qualified his 'incommensurability' thesis, though he continues to maintain that there is no neutral observation language. Communication is by no means impossible between men with rival paradigms. 'Both their everyday and most of their scientific world and language are shared. Given that much in common, they should be able to find out a great deal about how they differ.'[32] Each can try to see a phenomenon from the other's viewpoint, and eventually even anticipate how he would interpret it. The problem, says Kuhn, is like that of translation between two language communities, which is difficult but not impossible. This analogy allows Kuhn to retain some vestiges of his idea of 'conversion' – for a person can go beyond translation to the actual adoption of a new language in which he thinks and speaks.

4. *The 'rationality' of paradigm-choice*. Kuhn objects strongly to the charge of irrationality. If science is not rational, he asks, what is? But to understand what scientific rationality really requires, we have to look at science with care. Kuhn reminds his critics that he always has maintained that there are 'good reasons' and 'hardheaded arguments' for choosing paradigms. In his Postscript he spells out more fully the values which are shared by all scientists:

Probably the most deeply held values concern predictions: they should be accurate; quantitative predictions are preferable to qualitative ones; whatever the margin of permissible error, it should be consistently satisfied in a given field; and so on. There are also, however, values to be used in judging whole theories: they must, first and foremost, permit puzzle-formulation and solution; where possible they should be simple, self-consistent, and plausible, compatible, that is, with other theories currently deployed. (I now think it a weakness of my original text that so little attention is given to such values as internal and external consistency in considering sources of crisis and factors in theory choice).[33]

Kuhn insists, however, that these shared values provide no auto-

Paradigms in Science

matic rules for paradigm choice, since there is inevitable *variation in individual judgment* in applying them. Moreover, not all persons will assign the same relative weights among these values. After stating that debates over fundamental theories do not resemble logical or mathematical proofs, Kuhn concludes:

> Nothing about that relatively familiar thesis implies either that there are no good reasons for being persuaded or that those reasons are not ultimately decisive for the group. Nor does it even imply that the reasons for choice are different from those usually listed by philosophers of science: accuracy, simplicity, fruitfulness, and the like. What it should suggest, however, is that such reasons function as values and that they can thus be differently applied, individually and collectively, by men who concur in honouring them. If two men disagree, for example, about the relative fruitfulness of their theories, or if they agree about that but disagree about the relative importance of fruitfulness and, say, scope in reaching a choice, neither can be convicted of a mistake. Nor is either being unscientific. There is no neutral algorithm for theory-choice, no systematic decision procedure which, properly applied, must lead each individual in the group to the same decision.[34]

Kuhn offers a pragmatic justification for this variability of individual judgment. For if everyone abandoned an old paradigm when it first ran into difficulties, all effort would be diverted from systematic development to the pursuit of anomalies and the search for alternatives – almost all of which would be fruitless. On the other hand, if no one took alternative paradigms seriously, radically new viewpoints would never be developed far enough to gain acceptance. Variations in judgment allow a distribution of risks, which no uniform rules could achieve. Yet the fact that there are agreed values encourages communication and the eventual emergence of a scientific consensus. Finally, these values provide standards in terms of which one can see genuine progress as one looks at a succession of theories in history. 'That is not a relativist's position, and it displays the sense in which I am a convinced believer in scientific progress.'[35] Kuhn thus denies the allegations of irrationality and subjectivism.

Some of Kuhn's critics are still far from satisfied in this regard. Thus Shapere, in a review of Kuhn's recent writings, repeats his earlier epithets:

It is a viewpoint as relativistic, as antirationalistic, as ever . . . He seems to want to say that there are paradigm-independent considerations which constitute rational bases for introducing and accepting new paradigms; but his use of the term 'reasons' is vitiated by his considering them to be 'values', so that he seems not to have gotten beyond his former view after all. He seems to want to say that there is progress in science; but all grounds of assessment again apparently turn out to be 'values', and we are left with the same old relativism . . . The point I have tried to make is not merely that Kuhn's is a view which denies the objectivity and rationality of the scientific enterprise; I have tried to show that the arguments by which Kuhn arrives at this conclusion are unclear and unsatisfactory.[36]

Shapere does not define 'rationality', but he evidently identifies it with rule-governed choice. Kuhn is called 'anti-rationalistic', it seems, because he still holds that the choice of paradigms is not unequivocally specified by the values accepted throughout the scientific community. Such name-calling, however, sheds little light on the question of how choices in science are or should be made.

5. CRITERIA OF ASSESSMENT IN SCIENCE

In this section, a view of criteria for scientific choice is proposed which incorporates what I take to be the most significant insights of Kuhn's reformulated position and the most important contributions of his critics. Such a position may be less exciting than either the early empiricists' 'objectivism' or the 'subjectivism' which many readers found in Kuhn's first edition. But hopefully it can better represent an accurate description of what scientists actually do and a fruitful prescription for the continuation of the distinctive achievements of science. Its implications for the critique of religion are analysed in the next chapter.

I will distinguish the following aspects of science:

(1) observations,

(2) theories and theoretical models,

(3) 'research traditions' (Kuhn) or 'research programmes' (Lakatos), over a span of time, embodied in key examples ('exemplars'), and

(4) metaphysical assumptions about the nature of entities in the world.

In subsequent chapters I will use the term 'paradigm' to refer to the third component above, namely, a tradition transmitted through historical exemplars, but in this section I will avoid using the term because Kuhn used it in a variety of senses in his earlier writing. Exemplars have an important practical function in this scheme; as key examples, rather than explicit rules, they serve to initiate the student into the methods of attacking a problem which are accepted within a research tradition, and they guide the projected research programme of a particular scientific community. But exemplars do not determine the criteria for theory choice, and they can be considered separately from metaphysical assumptions. Traditions influence the type of model which is proposed in a new situation. Particular theoretical models (such as the billiard ball model of a gas) are treated here along with the theories which they generate and by which they are tested. A number of my conclusions in the first part of this chapter can now be applied within this scheme.

First, *all data are theory-laden, but rival theories are not incommensurable*. There is no pure observation language; the distinction between theory and observation is relative, pragmatic and context-dependent. But protagonists of rival theories can seek a common core of overlap in observation languages, on a level closer to agreed observations to which both can retreat. This seems a more accurate way of describing communication concerning observations during basic controversies (such as those over relativity and quantum theory) than Kuhn's recent analogy of 'translation', which assumes no common terms. It also allows more continuity and carry-over at the level of observations and laws before and after a revolution, and hence a more cumulative history, than Kuhn and Feyerabend recognize.

Something rather like a '*gestalt* switch' does occur in moving from one comprehensive theory to another. Different features of the phenomenon are selected for attention; new problems, new variables, new relationships are of interest. A familiar situation is seen in a new way. Further, it may be necessary to challenge and reinterpret the interpretive component of observations; to that extent, the data can be said to change. But this usually involves a retreat to observations whose interpretive component is not in doubt. Even in a *gestalt* switch, after all, there are lines in the picture which remain unchanged. Unlike a *gestalt* switch, however, there are in science criteria for favouring one interpretation over another – though I will suggest that in the very early stages, when a comprehensive theory of wide scope is first proposed, these criteria seldom yield definitive conclusions.

Second, *comprehensive theories are highly resistant to falsification, but observation does exert some control over them.* There are no 'crucial experiments' which can be specified in advance. But the degree of vulnerability to counter-instances varies considerably among the various components of science. If unsupported by a theory, a law stating relationships between variables which are relatively 'observable' will be thrown into question by a few persistent discrepancies. Theories, especially comprehensive ones, are more resistant to falsification, but an accumulation of anomalies, or of *ad hoc* modifications having no independent experimental or theoretical basis, cannot be tolerated indefinitely. An accepted comprehensive theory is overthrown not primarily by discordant data but by an alternative theory; we should visualize not a two-way confrontation of theory and experiment, but a complex confrontation of rival theories and a body of data of varying degrees of susceptibility to reinterpretation. A research programme is even more resistant to change than a theory, but may eventually be abandoned in favour of a new programme which has greater promise of explaining known data, resolving anomalies, and predicting novel phenomena.

Commitment to a research tradition and *tenacity* in a research programme are scientifically fruitful (on this Kuhn and Lakatos agree). Only if scientists stick with a programme and do not abandon it too readily will its potentialities be systematically explored and exploited. What balance between criticism and commitment is possible and desirable? Here Kuhn's revised picture of normal science allows for considerable diversity within a scientific community – including the presence of rival small groups and competing 'schools of thought'. Popper's advocacy of 'continual criticism' ('we can break out of our frameworks at any time') and Feyerabend's plea for a plurality of basic alternatives in every field at all times ('proliferation of theories', 'perpetual revolution') seem unrealistic and, even if they could be achieved, wasteful of scarce scientific manpower. There is both historical and strategic justification for Kuhn's view that, for most scientists, fruitful work is achieved within a framework of accepted assumptions, except when major difficulties in dominant theories are evident.

Third, *there are no rules for choice between research programmes, but there are independent criteria of assessment.* Criteria are indeed acquired more from studying past exemplars than from learning explicit principles; but they are common to many exemplars and can be stated apart from any of them. A scientist usually has some training in several related fields and some familiarity with their exemplars; his criteria are not dependent on one tradition alone.[37] As outlined earlier, the most important criteria are simplicity, coherence, and the extent and variety of supporting experimental evidence (including precise predictions and the anticipation of the discovery of novel types of phenomena). But there are no rules, no specific instructions, that is, for the unambiguous application of the criteria; there is, in Kuhn's words, 'no systematic decision procedure which must lead each individual in the group to the same decision'. Yet the criteria provide what Kuhn calls 'shared values' and 'good reasons' for choice; they are 'important determinants of group behaviour, even though the members of the group do not apply them in the same way'.

In *the very early stages*, when a comprehensive theory and its development into a research programme are first proposed, empirical criteria seldom have a predominant role. To return once more to our historical example: in the history of the theory of relativity, the Michelson-Morley experiment did not play the determinative part most textbooks assign to it. In point of fact, all of the experimental evidence on which Einstein drew had been available for fifty years; he was unaware of the Michelson-Morley results until considerably later. He was interested primarily in simplicity and coherence – in particular, the symmetry of the forms of the equations for electrical and magnetic fields in motion.[38] The variability of individual weighting among various criteria, which Kuhn describes, is also most noticeable in the early stages of a new theory. Thus the inconsistency between Bohr's quantum theory and the assumptions of classical physics worried some physicists very much when it was first proposed, whereas others thought this inconsistency of little importance compared to the accuracy of the predictions which it yielded.

The criteria for assessing theories are relevant to the *evaluation of research programmes*, but they cannot be applied in any rigorous way. The decision to abandon an accepted programme will depend on judgments of the seriousness of the anomalies, inconsistencies, and unsolved puzzles in the old programme (these are sometimes more important than Lakatos admits), and the promise of a proposed new programme. As Lakatos maintains, there are no clear-cut rules for such decisions, and there are risks in either changing programmes too precipitously or too reluctantly. The decision may be vindicated only decades later – which does not help much during the scientific controversy itself. Yet because there are accepted criteria common to all scientists the decision can be discussed and reasons set forth, and an eventual consensus can be expected.

Theories and programmes, then, are not verified or falsified, but *assessed by a variety of criteria*. Expecially in the early stages of controversial theories of great generality, and in the decision to abandon a well-developed research programme in favour of a promising but undeveloped new one, the assessment is an act of personal judgment. In such circumstances the scientist is more like a judge weighing the evidence in a difficult case than like a computer performing a calculation. The judgment cannot be reduced to formal rules, yet it is subject to rational argument and evaluation by commonly agreed criteria. The impossibility of specifying explicit rules is one of the reasons why editors of scientific journals and panels awarding research grants must have considerable discretionary power in evaluating new ideas.

Finally, *metaphysical assumptions* are one stage further from direct empirical verification or falsification, yet even these are not totally immune to change. I agree with Kuhn that the scientist does have beliefs about the kinds of entity there are in the world, and does have ontological commitments (and not merely methodological commitments for the sake of a fruitful research strategy, as Lakatos would have it). Because Newtonian mechanics was spectacularly successful, physicists not only used it as an exemplar of what a theory should be like, but also took its categories as indicative of the constituents of the universe. Additional assumptions were made concerning regularity, causality, action-at-a-distance and other basic features of the world. The same conceptual categories and presuppositions proved to be powerful tools in many fields, from astronomy to chemistry and biology. Less legitimately, perhaps, these metaphysical commitments were extended to a total world-view of reality as matter in motion.

But several things can happen to change the dominance of a set of metaphysical assumptions. The selection of the particular features of the research programme which had been assumed to be responsible for its success may be reconsidered; the emphasis may be placed instead on other features of the programme. Again, research programmes in one field – or in several fields – may be replaced by new programmes using very different basic concepts. Interest may also shift to new scientific fields, or to new areas of human experience; the earlier extension of metaphysical assumptions from one field, as wider interpretive categories for a total world-view, may then be questioned. In the course of history such assumptions have changed – at least partially in response to changes in science, though also in response to changing views of other area of human experience.

The position I have presented is consistent with the *critical realism* defended in Chapter 3 above. Naive realism is not plausible if the history of science provides evidence of major paradigm shifts rather than simple cumulation and convergence. Thus Mary Hesse writes:

> The history of science has already sufficiently demonstrated that successive acceptable theories are often in radical conceptual contradiction with each other. The succession of theories of the atom, for example, exhibits no 'convergence' in descriptions of the nature of fundamental particles, but

oscillates between continuity and discontinuity, field conceptions and particle conceptions, and even speculatively among different topologies of space.[39]

On the other hand, there is in the history of science more continuity than one would expect from Feyerabend or from Kuhn's earlier work, in which truth is entirely relative to a succession of self-contained language systems dominated by diverse paradigms. I have argued that observations and basic laws are retained through paradigm-shifts, at least as limiting cases under specifiable circumstances; a new theory usually explains why the older theory was as good as it was and why its limitations became evident.

To summarize: the scheme I have outlined accepts the three 'subjective' theses that (1) all data are theory-laden, (2) comprehensive theories are highly resistant to falsification, and (3) there are no rules for choice between research programmes. It also preserves Kuhn's most distinctive contributions concerning paradigms: the importance of exemplars in the transmission of a scientific tradition, and the strategic value of commitment to a research programme. At the same time I have made three assertions which seem to me essential for the objectivity of science: (1) rival theories are not incommensurable, (2) observation exerts some control over theories, and (3) there are criteria of assessment independent of particular research programmes.

7

Paradigms in Religion

IN CHAPTER 4 above it was proposed that the data of religion are experiences and events which are interpreted by imaginative models. As scientific models lead to theories by which observations are ordered, so religious models lead to beliefs by which experiences are ordered. Beliefs, like theories, can be propositionally stated and systematically articulated. But can religious beliefs be tested against human experience, as scientific theories can be tested against observations? Are there any criteria for the assessment of religious beliefs?

In the first section of this chapter the influence of interpretation on experience in religion is explored, paralleling the discussion of the influence of theory on observation in the previous chapter. Then the debate over the falsifiability of religious beliefs is appraised in the light of our conclusions about falsifiability in science. Section 3 examines the role of commitment to religious paradigms, understood as traditions transmitted by historical exemplars. Thereafter some distinctive problems of religious belief are taken up: the character of religious faith, the problem of transcendence and the status of metaphysics. The final section is concerned with criteria of assessment and their limitations.

I. THE INFLUENCE OF INTERPRETATION ON EXPERIENCE

Positivist authors since Hume have held that experience starts from the passive reception of momentary, disconnected, uninterpreted sense-data. Experience, for the positivist, is the private, subjective awareness of sense qualities produced by physical stimuli from the external world. It should be evident that this is a theory of experience, rather than a description of human consciousness. I would advocate an alternative theory which identifies primary experience with pre-reflective awareness of the flow of living activity in the interaction of organism and environment. It is a product of something encountered and a being capable of apprehending and interpreting that encounter. In a growing child, the distinction of self and world arises gradually because of his selective interest and responsive activity. The being who experiences is an active agent in the world, not a passive recipient of data. The contributions of subject and object, in this view, are complex and never totally separable.[1]

Our experience is not purely *subjective*, since we cannot make of it what we will. It is at least in part a 'given' which we are powerless to alter, a demand upon us to which we must conform. We respond as beings participating in a wider world. But experience is not purely *objective*, for it is qualified by the memories, feelings and concepts of the experiencing subject. Perceptual error and illusion warn us that the senses can be deceptive. We learn to discriminate according to the reliability with which our expectations are confirmed as we act in the world, and we compare our judgments with those of other persons responding to a common world.

There is, in short, *no uninterpreted experience* of the sort which the positivist posits. We don't simply see; we 'see as'. In the act of perception, the irreducible 'data' are not isolated patches of colour or fragmentary sensations, but total patterns in which interpretation has already entered. Our experience is organized in the light of particular interests. Language itself also structures our experience in specific ways. Conceptual presuppositions are transmitted by culturally-provided words which give form to experience. What we count as 'given' depends on our conceptual framework and the interests which it serves. The positivist's quest for the certainty of an incorrigible foundation for knowledge cannot be satisfied. No sense-datum statement is free of conceptual commitments that might subsequently need revision. The distinction between experience and interpretation, like that between observation and theory in science, is relative and context-dependent.

I respond to a table, not to a set of sense-data. Relations, connections, transitions and changes are as much part of my experience as patches of colour. There is continuity and cumulative identity both in what is experienced and in the one who experiences, rather than a sequence of disconnected impressions. There is also a social context of experience which the positivist theory leaves out; critical comparison of judgments depends on interaction with others, as we saw in the case of science as a community of enquiry. The diversity of dimensions of experience arises jointly from the capacities of things encountered to sustain a diversity of relationships and from the diversity of purposes which I have in confronting them. I respond to the table as an object of use, of beauty, of value, etc.; it has a variety of capacities and contexts and I have a variety of purposes and ways of looking at it.

With this brief introduction, let us reflect on the two basic types of experience which were described in Chapter 5 above. *Numinous encounter* is characterized by awe, reverence, mystery and wonder. There is a sense of being grasped and laid hold of, and a conviction that one's response is evoked.[2] This pattern, we saw, is typically associated with worship and with personal models of the divine. *Mystical union*, on the other hand, is characterized by joy, serenity and peace. The mystic speaks of the unity of all things and the loss of individual identity. He practices meditation and tends to use impersonal models.

While the descriptions of their experiences given by mystics in various cultures have much in common, the attempts to specify *that which evokes* the experience diverge more strongly. In Vedanta Hinduism the interpretive framework is monistic and pantheistic; the goal is union with the impersonal absolute, which only in popular piety is represented in personal forms. Mysticism in the Judaeo-Christian tradition usually receives a theistic interpretation; the gulf between the human and the divine is transcended but not denied. The self is said to be united with, but not totally obliterated by, the infinite. A historical development from polytheism to monotheism has occurred in many world religions, accompanied by a weaving together of mystical and numinous strands, but there are notable exceptions. Therevada Buddhism is agnostic about the object of contemplation; nirvana is the disclosure of a spiritual state, not a personal God, though it does transcend the categories of natural existence.

Ninian Smart maintains that the difference between these accounts lies in *the way the experience is interpreted* rather than in the experience itself. He recognizes that there is no descriptive language which is doctrinally neutral. But higher-level descriptions employ 'concepts of high ramification' which derive their meaning from a complex system of doctrinal statements. 'The higher the degree of ramification, the less is the description guaranteed by the experience itself, and the more other ideas are presupposed.' Relatively unramified lower-level descriptions can be given, however, which do not employ the terminology of developed doctrinal systems, and at this level there is greater agreement among mystics of diverse traditions.[3]

But is religious experience definite enough to be even remotely comparable to scientific data? Observations in science, though never free from interpretation, are *reproducible* within a scientific community because the observation-procedures are reliable, the events being studied are lawful, and the phenomena are publicly accessible. Proponents of conflicting theories, as I argued, can retreat to a level of observation-statement whose theoretical assumptions are not at issue. Religious experience, by contrast, seems variable, elusive and private; it is influenced by emotions and feelings and by individual temperament and life history. To be sure, typical experiences are reproducible in particular religious communities, but the latter are usually more restricted in scope than particular scientific communities. And while there may be greater agreement among 'lower-level' descriptions of religious experience than among doctrinal interpretations, there remains considerable diversity even among the former.

If there is no uninterpreted experience, there can be *no immediate religious knowledge*, no 'self-authenticating' awareness of God, no incorrigible intuition for which finality can be claimed. For when interpretation is present there is always the possibility of misinterpretation, especially through wishful thinking which reads into experience more than is warranted. Nor can there be any certain inference from experience to a being who is its independent cause. The sense of confrontation, encounter, and unexpectedness are no guarantee of the existence of a source beyond us. The mystic's vision cannot certify the reality of its object. Any verbal statement about such experiences employs conceptual structures which are culturally conditioned. People describe religious experience in conformity with the historic tradition to which they belong.

The key question is whether in religion *the data exercise any control at all* on the interpretation. There is a tendency for any set of basic beliefs to produce experiences which can be cited in support of those beliefs, which are then self-confirming. Interpretive ideas influence the believer's expectations; a suggestible person may experience what he has been taught to experience. Interests and commitments profoundly influence the religious life of individuals and communities. With some interpretive assumptions, worship would suffer or cease; with others, corporate sensitivity and concern for worship would be heightened. As in art and literature, the participant's capacity for response influences the range and depth of his experience.

Ronald Hepburn maintains that a *theist* and an *atheist* can have identical experiences and yet interpret them differently. Even proponents of a naturalistic philosophy, he maintains, can undergo profound numinous experiences.[4] But I wonder whether the atheist's expectations may not influence his openness to such types of experience and diminish the seriousness with which he will take them. Mystical experience would tend to become a psychological curiosity to which little significance is attached. Could the contexts in which such experiences occur be sustained in isolation from any religious tradition? Would the necessary personal involvement be encouraged if they were understood to disclose nothing beyond man's own inner life?

It may be objected that by stressing religious experience I have made a *naturalistic interpretation* inescapable. Hepburn and others have noted that reports of religious experience resemble psychological reports. The statement 'I feel sad' is unfalsifiable; but it is immune to falsification only because it makes no claims about the world. Munz holds that all religious language is a symbolization of feeling-states, an expression of psychological attitudes. J. H. Randall and Santayana take religious images to be symbols of man's ideals and inner experience.[5] Does a concern for religious experience lead inescapably to such subjective views?

It should at least be clear that we are not forced on logical grounds to *reduce* statements about God to statements about human experience. The assertion 'God exists' does not mean 'men have religious experiences'. I pointed out earlier that the meaning of theoretical terms in science is not derived from observations alone. Statements about unobservable molecules cannot be reduced to statements about observable pressures and volumes. Similarly, even if observations of behaviour provide evidence for statements about another person's mental state, behavioural terms do not express exhaustively the meaning of mental terms. 'John is generous' is an assertion about his intentions as well as his actions. The positivist identification of 'meaning' with 'method of verification' must be rejected in each of these cases. The reduction of statements about God to statements about religious experience is as unnecessary as the reduction of statements about material objects to statements about sense experience.

I would conclude that *interpretive beliefs* are brought to religious experience as much as they are derived from it. There is a greater influence in religion than in science 'from the top down': from paradigms, through interpretive models and beliefs, to experience. But the influence 'from the bottom up', starting from experience, is not totally absent in religion. Although there is no neutral descriptive language, there are degrees of interpretation. Therefore religious beliefs, and even paradigms, are not totally incommensurable. There can be significant communication between paradigm communities. One cannot prove one's most fundamental beliefs, but one can try to show how they function in the interpretation of experience.

If we turn from numinous and mystical experience to *events in the world*, the data are more objective, but here also there is the possibility of *alternative interpretations*. In Chapter 4 above, Wisdom's discussion of 'seeing as' and Hick's analysis of 'experiencing as' were mentioned. In a similar vein Anders Jeffner has pointed out that human nature, the history of mankind, and events in the world offer to us 'ambiguous patterns' and 'uncertain *gestalts*' which can be experienced in more than one way. He acknowledges an interpretive element in all experience; especially in looking at the universe as a whole 'the facts of life can fall into different patterns'. Metaphors and indirect sentences 'evoke and express one of the possible experiences of ambiguous objects'. There is no neutral data which can resolve such ambiguities, for alternative interpretations systematically influence the way we experience the world.[6]

Does not this very *ambiguity of the evidence* count against theism? Would we not expect a personal God to have revealed himself more clearly? John Hick maintains that, on the contrary, a God who respects human freedom would not overwhelm us with indubitable evidence. If God wants our voluntary response and freely-given love, he must safeguard our autonomy and allow for a variety of interpretations of the world, rather than coercing and dominating us by revealing himself more directly. He veils himself to protect our independence, and his actions leave room for our uncompelled decision.[7] It might be added that the classical arguments (cosmological and teleological) may not be conclusive as proofs of the existence of God, and yet may be conducive to an experience of awe and wonder which is amenable to theistic interpretation.

We can deny that God is an immediate and *uninterpreted datum in experience*, as many mystics have held, without going to the opposite extreme of saying that God is *inferred without being experienced*, as defenders of the teleological and cosmological arguments have often held. To make God a hypothesis to be tested or a conclusion of an argument is to lose the experiential basis of religion. In my view God is known through *interpreted experience* of three kinds: religious experience, patterns in the world, and particular historical events (Chapter 8 below). Our knowledge of God is like knowledge of another self in being neither an immediate datum nor an inference.

Another self is not immediately experienced; it must express itself through various media of language and action which we interpret. Yet we do not merely infer that another self is present; as a precondition for taking words and gestures as expressions of purpose and intention we must already understand ourselves to be dealing with another self.[8] Members of a religious community similarly understand themselves to be dealing with God; such an understanding is so basic that it may seem almost as much a part of interpreted experience as encounter with another self. Yet many persons today do not understand themselves to be dealing with God. Because of the diversity of interpretations, I have used the phrase 'interpreting as' in the contemporary religious context in preference to Hick's phrase 'experiencing as', while recognizing that the difference is one of emphasis only. I will return to the comparison of knowledge of God and other selves at a later point.

2. ON THE FALSIFIABILITY OF BELIEFS

We ask now whether religious beliefs in the interpretation of the pattern of events in the world are *falsifiable*. Widely divergent answers have been given in the Great Falsification Debate touched off by Antony Flew. Flew's article starts from Wisdom's parable, to which I referred earlier, concerning the explorer who finds a clearing in the jungle and asserts: 'Some gardener must tend this plot.' When no gardener is ever seen, the man qualifies his assertion: 'But perhaps he is an invisible gardener.' In similar fashion, says Flew, theists so qualify every statement about God that it is *unfalsifiable* and hence is 'no longer an assertion at all'. Theism is a victim of 'the death by a thousand qualifications'.

Flew closes his essay with the much-debated challenge:

Now it often seems to people who are not religious as if there was no conceivable event or series of events the occurrence of which would be admitted by sophisticated religious people to be a sufficient reason for conceding 'There wasn't a God after all' or 'God does not really love us then' . . . I therefore put to the succeeding symposiasts the simple question, 'What would have to occur or to have occurred to constitute for you a disproof of the love of, or the existence of, God?'[9]

Flew makes *the specification of falsifying conditions* a criterion for meaningful assertions. It might better be taken as a criterion for factual assertions, since, as pointed out earlier, the equation of meaning with verifiability or falsifiability has been widely criticized. With this emendation, Flew can be taken to assert that a sentence is factual only if it is incompatible with some possible empirically identifiable state of affairs. If it is not in principle falsifiable by observations, it asserts nothing factually. Flew's challenge, then, is for the theist to specify the occurrences which would, as he puts it, 'constitute a disproof of' statements about God's love or existence.[10]

In response to this challenge some authors have replied that *the criterion of falsifiability is not applicable* to religious statements. They have developed further Wittgenstein's conviction that there are a variety of languages serving a diversity of human purposes and needs. Science is not the norm for all languages. Thus D. Z. Phillips construes theology as a conceptually autonomous language-game with its own rules. Evidence can be assessed only within a given linguistic framework; no external justification is needed or possible. Worship in particular is not a means to some other end, nor is it vindicated by its results. Religion is a practical 'form of life' with its own independent language and logic.[11]

According to Phillips, *all criteria are internal* to a language-using community. Diverse conceptions of rationality and intelligibility are determined by diverse linguistic frameworks. Indeed, what is taken to constitute reality will vary according to the universe of discourse. Assessment can occur within a linguistic frame, but the latter cannot itself be assessed. In adopting a religious form of life one's standards are transformed; what once was called failure may now be called success. Believer and unbeliever don't play the same game or appeal to the same criteria.

In the previous chapter I maintained that the choice among paradigms would be completely arbitrary if they were *incommensurable* and if there were *no shared criteria*. A similar objection can be raised against Phillips' avowal that all criteria are internal to particular religious communities. I have argued that religious traditions do make conflicting truth-claims; they do not merely offer 'different pictures which regulate personal life'. If religion were a self-contained language-game, it would be impervious to philosophical criticism, isolated from all other intellectual disciplines, and irrelevant to other areas of man's life. Moreover, the complete isolation of religious language would not be compatible with the extensive use of analogies drawn from other languages which I have earlier described. Is there not also more variety in the uses of language within a given religious community than Phillips' account portrays? Finally, no communication among different religious communities would be possible if the language of each were self-contained. The price of immunity to falsification would be the impossibility of discourse among adherents of diverse paradigms.[12]

Another type of response to Flew's challenge is to grant that there is no decisive falsification but to hold that *evidence does count for and against religious beliefs*. Basil Mitchell tells the now-familiar parable about a partisan who has met a stranger in the resistance movement during an enemy occupation; later the Stranger appears to be working for the enemy, but the partisan is convinced that the Stranger is really loyal. Whereas the explorer in Wisdom's parable was speculatively curious, Mitchell's partisan is personally involved; he has to act and his decisions have life-and-death seriousness. His belief is based on the initial evidence of personal encounter with the Stranger, and he does have a plausible explanation for the anomalous behaviour (the Stranger may want to secure information from the enemy).[13] Mitchell seems to be well on the way towards meeting Flew's challenge.

But could *an accumulation of negative evidence* lead the partisan to a reversal of his judgment? No, says Mitchell, for his commitment to trust the Stranger is an 'article of faith' rather than a 'provisional hypothesis':

'God loves men' resembles 'the Stranger is on our side' (and many other significant statements, e.g. historical ones) in not being conclusively falsifiable. They can both be treated in at least three different ways: (1) as provisional hypotheses to be discarded if experience tells against them; (2) as significant articles of faith; (3) as vacuous formulae (expressing, perhaps, a desire for reassurance) to which experience makes no difference and which make no difference to life.

The Christian, once he has committed himself, is precluded by his faith from taking up the first attitude: 'Thou shalt not tempt the Lord thy God'. He is in constant danger, as Flew has observed, of slipping into the third. But he need not; and if he does, it is a failure in faith as well as in logic.[14]

Mitchell says that 'pain and suffering do count against the assertion that God loves man' but they do not 'count decisively' for the person who has committed himself to belief in God. Mitchell thus partially satisfies Flew's demand: there is evidence for and against religious beliefs. But he seems to concede Flew's crucial point: no amount of evidence could lead to the abandonment of religious beliefs which are 'articles of faith'.

Others have gone further in meeting Flew's conditions. Crombie and Hick say that pointless and irredeemable suffering *would count decisively* against the assertion that God is merciful.[15] They acknowledge, however, that only in the hereafter could we determine whether suffering is irredeemable; reference to 'the world to come' specifies conditions for verification in principle, but not in practice. Howard Burkle, on the other hand, says that the total pattern of evidence now available, for and against, *does count decisively*:

> Within such a framework contradictory evidence can count decisively against in two senses. (1) It can contribute to a total pattern of negative evidence *tending* to falsify and obligating the believer to dissent if the evidence grows strong enough. Here evidence is decisive as part of a whole . . . (2) It can function as *the* piece of evidence that completes the tendency towards decision and precipitates dissent.[16]

While I am in agreement with Burkle's conclusion, I would want to go further than he does in questioning Flew's challenge itself. Let us now examine it in the light of my remarks in the previous chapter.

First, *the demand for the specification of falsifying conditions seems unreasonable*, since it cannot be met by scientific theories, especially those of great generality. We have seen that no 'crucial experiment' can be specified in advance for deciding with finality between two comprehensive theories. One hypothesis alone cannot be tested against one piece of empirical evidence. Rather, a whole network of concepts and assumptions is tested at once. Discordant data can be accommodated by modification of auxilliary hypotheses or *ad hoc* adjustments, or they can be set to one side as anomalies. The kind of 'qualification' to which Flew objects occurs frequently in the history of science (though one might legitimately object if they added up to 'a thousand qualifications').

Second, *empirical evidence is nevertheless not irrelevant*. Phillips seems to accept Flew's contention that all statements fall into two classes: (1) empirical statements whose falsifying conditions can be specified, and (2) nonempirical statements to which evidence is irrelevant. But if the conclusions of the previous chapter are correct, most components of science fall somewhere between these two extremes. There is increasing resistance to falsification as one moves from simple laws to limited theories, comprehensive theories, paradigms and finally metaphysical assumptions. Yet at none of these levels, I have urged, can an accumulation of counter-evidence be completely ignored. If a religious tradition is thought of as analagous to a research tradition, the cumulative weight of evidence cannot be dismissed.

Third, *comprehensive systems of belief are not falsified by discordant data but replaced by promising alternatives*. In the absence of alternatives, modifications can usually be made in accepted interpretive frameworks. In discussing the overthrow of comprehensive scientific theories, I intimated that we should picture not a two-way confrontation of theory with falsifying data, but a three-way confrontation of rival theories with a body of data of varying degrees of susceptibility to reinterpretation. In the religious case, some forms of atheism may start as purely negative protests against theism rather than as positive endorsements of an alternative position; but as soon as systematic reflection is attempted, atheism develops its own naturalistic beliefs and its own interpretation of religious experience. Abandoning one set of fundamental beliefs thus involves at least implicit acknowledgment of possible alternatives, even if one reserves judgment about them.

Fourth, *there are no rules for choice between paradigms but there are criteria independent of particular paradigms*. Past research traditions and future research programmes are not verified or falsified, I have said, but assessed by a variety of criteria which are not paradigm-dependent. Yet the application of the criteria is not unambiguous and is a matter of individual judgment. There are no rules which determine when to abandon an accepted research tradition. I will in a later section propose that there are likewise criteria but not rules for the assessment of religious paradigms; reasons for or against abandoning a tradition can be given.

Religious beliefs, in short, are *highly resistant to falsification,* but *the cumulative weight of evidence does count decisively* for or against them in the long run, in comparison with alternative interpretations. Men do and should modify or abandon their beliefs in the light of their experience. The theist can try to meet a weaker but more defensible form of Flew's challenge. He can admit that theistic belief would be unreasonable in the absence of the kinds of experience listed earlier: mystical and numinous encounter, reconciliation, key historical events, order and creativity in the world. The theist must also be able to provide some kind of account of the counter-evidence, such as evil and suffering, as we shall see. If evidence were irrelevant, there would be no way of detecting illusion, and beliefs would be totally incorrigible.

The view I am advocating may be clarified by distinguishing it from the position advanced in a recent response to Flew by John F. Miller. Both science and religion, he maintains, are based on '*first-order principles*' which cannot be falsified:

> As in religion with its first-order non-falsifiable statements, *nothing is allowed to count against* these important first-order scientific principles which have been discussed (causality, determinism, the principle of the rectilinear propagation of light, the law of the conservation of energy). Therefore, religion and science are logically similar in this respect: both have within their conceptual frameworks or world-views non-verifiable principles of a first-order status which are principles *in accordance with which* inferences are drawn and evidence is adduced.[17]

The examples that Miller provides are somewhat diverse, but none of them seems to me totally unfalsifiable in the absolute sense which he claims. To be sure, the principle of conservation of energy was preserved in the face of discordant data by *ad hoc* amendments such as the postulation of the neutrino, as I have noted. But a prolonged accumulation of anomalies or *ad hoc* amendments would, I believe, have brought about reformulations of the principle itself or qualification of its universality. All physicists do *not* assume that the principle of determinism must hold in the atomic domain, as I indicated in Chapter 5 above; Miller bases his case for quantum determinism largely on Planck's writings, which represent a minority position among scientists and philosophers today. In general, Miller adopts a more 'subjective' view of science than I have advocated. He says that 'science is a picture preference' in which 'we choose to see the world in a particular way'; our conceptual frameworks determine 'the evidence', not *vice versa*. Science and religion, he concludes, are 'logically similar' in that the 'first principles' of *both* are *unfalsifiable*.

In a reply to Miller, King-Farlow and Christensen go to the opposite extreme, asserting that science and religion are similar because *both* are in principle *falsifiable*. 'This will involve accepting analogies between theological statements and so-called hypotheses, insofar as the latter are propositions held and put forward in a somewhat tentative spirit with a view to explaining what we experience.' These authors urge an attitude of great tentativeness, tolerance and openness, which they identify with the acceptance of the falsifiability of even one's most basic beliefs. They hold that 'falsifiable theism' can meet Flew's challenge.[18]

Norman Siefferman, on the other hand, replies to Miller by making a strong contrast between *falsifiable* scientific statements and *unfalsifiable* religious ones – much as Flew himself might have done. Siefferman claims that in science, but not in religion, a conflict between theory and observation leads directly to falsification. 'Since the conservation law was formulated from empirical evidence, it can be falsified by it.'[19] This, too, strikes me as an over-simplified account of the process of assessment in science as well as in religion.

My complaint with all three of these analyses is that they treat 'falsifiability' and 'unfalsifiability' as absolute and mutually exclusive categories. I have urged that even within science there are *degrees of resistance to falsification*, with paradigms and metaphysical assumptions most resistant but by no means totally invulnerable in the long run to cumulative empirical evidence. I would assign scientific paradigms a position near the middle of the 'falsifiability' spectrum – not at the extreme of 'objectivity' or 'falsifiability' as King-Farlow and Christensen as well as Siefferman assume. Religious paradigms I would assign towards the 'subjective' or 'unfalsifiable' end of the spectrum, because of the influence of interpretation on experience – but not at the extreme of 'subjectivity' (in the sense of immunity to evidence) which both Miller and Siefferman assume. Thus in comparing science and religion on a spectrum of degrees of resistance to falsification, I can point to *both* similarities and contrasts – whereas those who use only two boxes, labelled 'falsifiable' and 'unfalsifiable', have no option but to view science and religion either as *similar* (assigned to the same box, whichever it is), or *contrasting* (assigned to different boxes). I believe that recent work in the philosophy of science here casts significant light on the protracted debate about falsifiability in religion.

3. COMMITMENT TO PARADIGMS

Let us now examine more closely some parallels between commitment to a religious paradigm and commitment to a scientific paradigm, understood as a research tradition transmitted by key historical examples or exemplars. First we may recall *the importance of the community* of scientists interacting over a period of time. Neither religion nor science is an individual affair. Religion is corporate; even the contemplative mystic is influenced by a historical tradition. No one adheres to science or religion in general; the initiate joins a particular community and adopts its modes of thought and action.

Next, *crucial historical events* are central in the transmission of a tradition. Newton's work in mechanics served as exemplar for classical physics. The key events remembered by a community help to define its self-identity. Kuhn seems to hold that the exemplars are edited and perhaps idealized versions of historical accomplishments which appear in textbooks, rather than the actual historical events themselves. Events in the lives of Moses, Buddha and Christ play somewhat similar roles in the self-definition of religious communities. It is the edited narratives in the scriptures and the often idealized 'lives of saints' which are influential – though here the attempt to recover authentic history is itself religiously significant, despite the limits of such an endeavour (biblical criticism, the quest for the historical Jesus, etc.). Furthermore, religious traditions, unlike scientific ones, are often totally and explicitly organized around the memory of their historical exemplars as individual persons. Particular aspects of their lives serve as norms for the community's life and thought.

I have discussed elsewhere the status of events in history which are taken by a religious community to be *revelatory*.[20] I cited the view of several theologians that there is no uninterpreted revelation; we are given not revealed propositions, but a human record of historical events understood to have involved both man and God. The locus of God's action is not the dictation of an inerrant book, but the lives of individuals and communities. Revelatory events are recognized today by their ability to illuminate present experience; the special event enables us to see what is universally present. The past provides clues for the interpretation of the present; particular points in history disclose the powers at work throughout history. The exemplars of a religious community are thus more determinative of its ongoing life than those of a scientific community, as we will see in the next chapter.

It is sometimes said that the *commitment* characteristic of religion contrasts with the *tentativeness* of science. We have noted Mitchell's contention that religious beliefs are 'articles of faith', not 'tentative hypotheses'. But the contrast is not as great if religious traditions are compared with research traditions rather than with scientific hypotheses.[21] In the previous chapter I concluded that the scientist does have a commitment to a tradition and legimately sticks to it with considerable tenacity, exploring its potentialities rather than abandoning it too readily. It will be recalled that for Lakatos this commitment is a deliberate methodological decision; the 'core' of a programme is treated as unfalsifiable, in order to develop its 'positive heuristic'. In Kuhn's account, which seems to me more plausible, the commitment arises from the scientific community's unconscious assumptions, which influence all its ways of thinking.

Lakatos' view of scientific commitment as a deliberate methodological decision might be compared with *voluntarist views of religious faith*. William James speaks of 'the will to believe'; a person must act as if religious beliefs were true in order to live out their positive possibilities. F. R. Tennant refers to the sustained effort of the will required in any voyage of discovery; religious faith, he says, is like the deliberate decision to undertake and carry through a research project.[22] Again, in the interests of practical effectiveness a man may resolve to act decisively, even when the evidence is incomplete; perpetual suspended judgment would paralyze action. I wonder, however, whether religious faith can be adequately represented as a purely pragmatic methodological decision. I suggest that, as in the scientific case, there are ontological commitments present in religion; in the absence of concern for the truth of one's beliefs, the path would be open to the arbitrary adoption of useful fictions. William James himself acknowledged that he should have spoken of 'the right to believe' rather than 'the will to believe', for he was aware of the danger that wishful thinking can restrict one's openness to new evidence.

In *religious faith* there are of course distinctive attitudes which are not present in commitment to a scientific tradition. In the biblical view, faith is personal trust, confidence and loyalty. Like faith in a friend or faith in a doctor, religious faith is not 'blind faith', for it is closely tied to experience. But it does entail risk and vulnerability in the absence of logical proof. Marriage is 'a venture of faith', not simply because its success is not predictable, but because it requires trust and self-commitment. Biblical faith is also 'faithfulness' and 'fidelity'. But all of these attitudes presuppose beliefs; one cannot trust God unless one believes he exists. As H. H. Price has shown, 'belief in' a person is both an expression of attitudes and an affirmation of beliefs about him ('belief that'); it is not reducible to either personal attitudes or propositional beliefs alone.[23]

Participation in a religious tradition also demands a more total *personal involvement* than occurs in science. Religious questions are of ultimate concern, since the meaning of one's existence is at stake. Religion asks about the final objects of a person's devotion and loyalty, for which he will sacrifice other interests if necessary. Too detached an attitude may cut a person off from the very kinds of experience which are religiously most significant. Reorientation and reconciliation are transformations of life-pattern affecting all aspects of personality, not intellect alone. Religious writings use the language of actors, not the language of spectators. Religious commitment, then, is a self-involving personal response, a serious decision implicating one's whole life, a willingness to act and suffer for what one believes in.

Is there in religion an *absolute commitment* which makes evidence irrelevant? Is total trust compatible with self-criticism and acknowledgment of the possibility of error? To the believer, disbelief may appear to be 'faithlessness', disloyalty and personal betrayal. 'True faith' is shown by complete trust even in adverse circumstances. Job could say, 'Though he slay me, yet will I trust in him.' St Paul could proclaim that 'neither death nor life . . . nor height, nor depth, nor any other creature, shall be able to separate us from the love of God, which is in Christ Jesus our Lord' (Rom. 8.39). Such passages express the conviction that even the personal experience of evil is not incompatible with religious faith. But does this imply that beliefs have no experiential basis or that they are immune to criticism?

I would submit that religious commitment can indeed be combined with *critical reflection*. Commitment alone without enquiry tends to become fanaticism or narrow dogmatism; reflection alone without commitment tends to become trivial speculation unrelated to real life. Perhaps personal involvement must alternate with reflection on that involvement, since worship and critical enquiry at their most significant levels do not occur simultaneously. It is by no means easy to hold beliefs for which you would be willing to die, and yet to remain open to new insights; but it is precisely such a combination of commitment and enquiry that constitutes religious maturity.[24]

If *faith* were simply the acceptance of revealed propositions or assent to propositions, it would be incompatible with *doubt*. But if faith means trust and commitment, it is compatible with considerable doubt about particular interpretations. Faith does not automatically turn uncertainties into certainties. What it does is take us beyond the detached speculative outlook which prevents the most significant sorts of experience; it enables us to live and act amid the uncertainties of life without pretensions of intellectual or moral infallibility. But it does not give us wisdom or virtue transcending the limitations of human existence. Doubt frees us from illusions of having captured God in a creed; it calls into question every religious symbol. We are dislodged from all the attempted securities on which we rely, including certainties of belief.

Self-criticism is called for if we acknowledge that no church, book, or creed is infallible, and no formulation is irrevocable. The claim of any human institution or theological system to finality must be questioned if we are to avoid absolutizing the relative. The prophets of all ages have reserved their harshest criticisms for their own religious communities. The distinctive character of commitment to a religious paradigm in short does not exclude critical reflection. In Chapter 8 below we will look further at the nature of the Christian paradigm.

4. DISTINCTIVE PROBLEMS OF RELIGIOUS BELIEF

I wish next to take up some possible objections arising from distinctive features of religious belief. First, can beliefs used in the interpretation of experience say anything about *transcendence*? Can models drawn from the finite world ever give more than a finite God who would not be a fitting object of devotion and worship? Can experience tell us about that which lies beyond experience?

In answering such objections, we must distinguish among meanings of transcendence. God is variously said to transcend (1) human thought, (2) human experience, (3) space and time, and (4) the world. Concerning the first, which is a form of *epistemological transcendence*, it is not illogical to say that God can be partially but not exhaustively represented in human thought.[25] If God were totally incomprehensible, or if the idea of God were self-contradictory, no intelligible statement about him could be made. One cannot conceive of the inconceivable, or worship a completely unknowable X. But one can acknowledge that models are not literal pictures, and that concepts are limited and culturally conditioned. Similarly it is not inconsistent to say that God is partially known through human experience but is not simply a dimension of experience. I indicated earlier that such an assertion is not unlike the assertion that electrons are known through observations but are not themselves observable. We can then say that God transcends thought and experience without implying that he is totally unknowable. The numinous experience of mystery and awe lends support to just this combination of ideas.

God is also said to *transcend time*. The idea of God as 'timeless', in the sense of static, unchanging, and unrelated to the temporal world, accords with neither biblical religion nor the process metaphysics which I would defend. But if God is 'everlasting' (Whitehead), I see no inherent theological or philosophical difficulties in such temporal transcendence. *Transcendence of space* is more problematic, but it would not be inconsistent to hold that God is everywhere present but lacks the spatial predicates of observable objects, such as size and location, which specify spatial limits. It would not be self-contradictory to believe that God is infinite, even though one could not encounter him in his infinity. Even in mathematics there are infinite sets (e.g. the real numbers) which can never be experienced as a totality.[26]

The most important question, then, is what it would mean to say that God *transcends the world*. Absolute transcendence would mean that God is totally independent of the world, a self-sufficient being unaffected by the world. A more limited transcendence, however, is compatible with divine immanence, namely the freedom of both God and the world to be themselves and yet to participate in each other in reciprocity. God and world could be inseparable but not identical. Evil and moral ambiguity in the world prevent us from identifying it with God. Grace and reconciliation are experienced as a power not our own; holiness is confronted as judgment over against us.

I will later suggest that God's creativity is *immanent* throughout the cosmic process, not an intervention from outside. God as the creative spirit and the ultimate order which makes process possible is the supreme power on which all things depend for their existence, but this is a power which evokes the response of the creatures, not an omnipotent predetermination which would deny their freedom. Transcendence, then, is not primarily priority in space and time (God as outside or before the world) but priority in status and role, in freedom and everlasting purpose, in holiness and righteousness.

Our *knowledge of other selves* provides at least partial analogies for several of these types of transcendence. We ascribe to another person a non-observable self which transcends our direct experience of his body and behaviour. Selfhood is not fully describable by the attributes predicated of objects in space and time.[27] A person is an agent as well as an activity, a centre of thought, intentionality and decision, who can reveal himself to us in deliberate communication. But knowledge of another person is mediated through his body and behaviour. In the following chapter I will ask whether an agent without a body is conceivable, or whether we should think of the world as in some sense God's 'body'. In that context I will examine distinctions between the language of 'actions' and the language of 'events'.

I will note here, however, that the same empiricist assumptions which exclude the existence of God also lead to *inadequate views of the self*. Hume, for example, maintained that all we are aware of are separate ideas and impressions. The self, he said, is a bundle of perceptions, formed from a succession of discontinuous sensations passively received. There is no enduring self as an active agent, according to Hume. For Ayer, the self is an abstract logical construction from sense experience. Ryle, in turn, wants to reduce all language about selves to language about behaviour. I will be maintaining, on the contrary, that the language of selfhood is distinctive. But this does not require the adoption of the mind-body dualism which Ryle attacks – nor, correspondingly, is a God-world dualism the only alternative to naturalistic reductionism.

In addition to these objections to the idea of transcendence, there are objections to the *metaphysical systems* in which religious beliefs are usually embedded. I have said that religious beliefs are relevant primarily to the interpretation of religious experience, patterns in the world and revelatory events in the life of communities. Beyond this, such beliefs are applicable to other personal and social life-situations; the data to which they direct attention are pre-eminently the experiences of active selves in decision – in love and hate, joy and tragedy, life and death, justice and injustice. But religious beliefs also provide a wider interpretive framework; they yield clues for a coherent view of diverse types of experience. They contribute to over-all metaphysical systems which claim to provide categories for the interpretation of all reality. Metaphysics is a sort of large-scale language-map integrating and unifying many different types of language, including those of science and religion.[28] But three kinds of objections have been raised:

1. *Metaphysical systems yield no predictions.* They seem to be even more difficult to falsify than religious beliefs. In contrast to research programmes in science, they do not lead to the prediction of particular novel phenomena, even 'in the long run'. For the metaphysician has tried to take all the major types of phenomena into account, and no radically new types are likely to occur. With only one universe as data, no comparisons are possible. However, I have suggested that although the metaphysical assumptions associated with scientific paradigms are extremely resistant to falsification, they are subject to some control through changes in theories and paradigms. Similar remarks could be made about the metaphysical assumptions in religious traditions. The assumptions are elaborated in metaphysical systems which are not proved or disproved, but are modified under the pressure of experience or replaced by alternative systems.

Thus I cannot accept E. D. Klemke's suggestion that religious assertions are unfalsifiable '*absolute presuppositions*'. He cites R. G. Collingwood's definition of metaphysics as the study of presuppositions which cannot be verified or falsified, such as 'every event has a cause'. Klemke thinks that the theologian, instead of trying to defend the statement 'God exists', should ask, 'What are the results within human experience of presupposing that God exists?'[29] But if we explore the results not only for action but also for thought, and especially for the interpretation of experience, then the implications of differing fundamental assumptions can be compared (unless, with Kant, it is held that there is a unique set of *a priori* presuppositions for all thought). Metaphysical assumptions, then, are not unrelated to empirical evidence, even though they yield no predictions.

2. *The God of metaphysics is not the God of religion.* It may be objected that the God of metaphysics is a theoretical construction produced by a speculative interest, not the object of devotion of a worshipping community. As I have presented it, however, metaphysics is a second-order reflection on experience – not identical with experience but not totally divorced from it either. Commitment and personal involvement, I have urged, need not exclude reflective enquiry. No sharp distinction between 'religious' and 'metaphysical' attributes of God can be made; only a God with certain kinds of attributes is an appropriate object of worship. Theologians who claim to eschew metaphysics may be only disguising their own metaphysical assumptions. Yet this objection can serve as a reminder of the temptation for abstract speculation to divorce itself from concrete human experience.

3. *Metaphysical systems distort the diversity of experience.* In attempting conceptual unity in an all-inclusive system of thought, the metaphysician tends to over-systematize. The danger here is that the conceptual framework developed in one area of experience will be artificially imposed on another area. It is partly in response to this danger that linguistic analysts have defended the autonomy of diverse language-games. I have urged, however, that because man searches for coherence, and because his various languages refer to a common world, we cannot rest content with a multiplicity of totally unrelated language-games.

But our goal must be modest, devoid of the pretensions of

grandiose system-building; any conceptual synthesis must be treated as partial and tentative. Human experience is indeed diverse, and each field of enquiry must have considerable autonomy. Metaphysical categories should allow for pluralism and variety. The connection of either science or religion with any metaphysical system should be flexible enough that the integrity of each field can be respected. Metaphysics is not a kind of super-science, since it must take into account other disciplines as well. But neither is it a super-theology imposing its framework on other fields of enquiry.

5. CRITERIA OF ASSESSMENT IN RELIGION

Before analysing criteria for cognitive claims, which have been our main concern in this chapter, we should look for a moment at possible criteria for non-cognitive functions. One such criterion is the ability of a religious tradition to *fulfil social and psychological needs*. Desirable social goals might include group unity, community stability and social harmony. Among psychological goals are self-understanding, maturity, and integration of personality. Religious faith may allay anxieties and impart a significant direction to an individual's life. Some authors have tried to derive an objective list of human needs from scientific analysis of man's nature; the fulfilment of such needs could then provide neutral criteria for assessing religious paradigms. It is dubious, however, whether formulations of such needs, and of their relative importance, can be made without value judgments which are culturally conditioned.

The results of religious beliefs in human life may also be judged by *ethical criteria*. 'By their fruits ye shall know them.' Religions could be assessed both by their professed ideals and by their capacity to inspire lives of compassion, creative love, and the enhancement of human relationships. William James claimed that religious experience is a source of moral power, inward peace, and saintliness. At the theoretical level, coherence among ethical values is supported by beliefs about the nature of reality and the destiny of man. More significantly, at the practical level, motivation to sustain action is a product of personal transformation and reorientation as well as commitment to a world-view. Religious beliefs can be judged by the ethical norms they uphold and their effectiveness in motivating ethical action.

Such ethical criteria are, of course, *paradigm-dependent*. Creative love and integration of personality are ideals endorsed by some traditions more strongly than others. There is an inescapable circularity in any attempt to assess the criteria of assessment. Criteria for non-cognitive functions are indeed internal to particular 'language-games' and relative to particular communities. The goals of the life-affirming Western tradition cannot be assumed in evaluating the pragmatic results of Eastern philosophies of life, for instance. We must turn, then, to the cognitive beliefs which are presupposed in these non-cognitive uses, even though the latter are in practice more important in the life of the religious community.

We ask, then, whether criteria for religious beliefs might parallel those for scientific theories. In any system of thought *simplicity* is desirable (e.g., minimum number of independent assumptions and conceptual categories); but it is seldom a major consideration in either science or religion. *Coherence* involves both internal consistency (the absence of contradictions) and systematic interrelatedness (the presence of connections and implications between statements). But *supporting evidence* is the most important criterion. Religious beliefs must give a faithful rendition of the areas of experience taken to be especially significant: religious and moral experience and key historical events. But they must also adequately interpret other events in our lives as active selves. Hence *extensibility* of application (fruitfulness) can be listed as an additional criterion. Finally, *comprehensiveness* in the coherent ordering of diverse types of experience within a systematic metaphysics is desirable, though, in my opinion, secondary to other criteria.

But in the *choice between paradigms*, the application of these criteria is even more indirect, ambiguous and debatable in religion than in science. Variations in individual judgment as to the relative weight which should be given to various criteria are more pronounced; some people seek systematic coherence above all else, while others stress adequacy to experience. Theravada Buddhism is remarkable for its simplicity, but perhaps at the price of comprehensiveness, since numinous experience and worship are less strongly represented than in other religions. Hinduism and Christianity include a richer interweaving of many strands, but at the price of simplicity. Among traditions there are also divergent convictions as to which types of experience are most significant. Between competing religious traditions there seem to be fewer common assumptions and less clear-cut common data than there are between competing scientific traditions, even during a scientific revolution.

In particular, religion lacks the *lower-level laws* which are characteristic of science. The terms of such laws are relatively close to observations, their theoretical components are not in dispute, and they are relatively vulnerable to falsification by counter-instances. These laws often survive scientific revolutions or undergo qualifications so that they can be retained under a restricted range of conditions; but sometimes newly formulated laws are historically important in the overthrow of a dominant paradigm. The absence of such laws in religion severely limits the extent to which data can exert some control over higher-level theories and paradigms. Statements which appear to be 'laws' (such as 'Sincere prayer will be answered') are too vague, and the terms are too elastic, for any precise application.

There are no rules for deciding when to abandon a paradigm in science, but *an eventual consensus* emerges – even though there may be rival paradigms for protracted periods, and no paradigm can be considered permanent. The emergence of consensus in religion seems an unrealizable goal. There are differences in cultural context which are intertwined with religious beliefs; hopefully any future global civilization will preserve considerable cultural diversity, and with it, religious pluralism. Among adherents of competing scientific paradigms there are common goals, standards and procedures, but among different religious communities such common methodological assumptions are seldom found.

In sum, each of the '*subjective*' features of science mentioned in the previous chapter is *more* evident in the case of religion: (1) the influence of interpretation on data, (2) the resistance of comprehensive theories to falsification, and (3) the absence of rules for choice among paradigms. Each of the corresponding '*objective*' features of science is *less* evident in the case of religion: (1) the presence of common data on which disputants can agree, (2) the cumulative effect of evidence for or against a theory, and (3) the existence of criteria which are not paradigm-dependent. It is clear that in all three respects religion is a more 'subjective' enterprise than science. But in each case there is a difference of degree – not an absolute contrast between an 'objective' science and a 'subjective' religion.

There are several reasons for stressing that in religion there are at least minimally present such 'objective' features as common experience, relevant evidence and common criteria. First, if it is true that an accepted paradigm is not falsified but replaced by an alternative, then the possibility of assessing a religious paradigm must in practice be compared with the possibility of assessing *alternative religious or naturalistic paradigms* – regardless of what the possibility of assessment in science may be. The most that one can expect of any set of beliefs is that it will make more sense of all the available evidence than alternative beliefs. The choice is not between religion and science, but between theism, pantheism and naturalism, let us say, as each is expressed in a particular historical tradition. No basic beliefs are capable of demonstrable proof. A set of beliefs must be considered as an organic network of interrelated ideas.

Second, the *self-criticism* of one's own basic beliefs is possible only if there are criteria which are not totally paradigm-dependent. Every person has such basic beliefs; the choice is not whether to hold them but which ones to hold. Decision and action express implicit if not explicit affirmations. Better, then, to hold beliefs critically than uncritically, even if there is ambiguity and risk in any such process of evaluation.

Third, *communication* between paradigm communities is impossible unless they partially share a common language. If there is no core of shared terms and no experiences common to both communities, their assertions are 'incommensurable' and no genuine discussion can occur. The further presence of shared criteria greatly enhances the fruitfulness of the interaction. I would maintain that persons in diverse traditions can appeal to facets of each other's experience and can discuss together their interpretive frameworks. Intelligible reasons can be offered, rather than arbitrary 'leaps of faith'.

The explorers in Wisdom's parable can converse. They confront together a common situation, in which each traces the patterns that he finds significant. Each underlines distinctive features whose cumulative effect has impressed him. As when literary critics evaluate a play, there are both data and criteria held in common which make possible a rational discussion even among those whose conclusions differ. There are no *proofs*, but there are good *reasons* for judgments which are not simply matters of personal taste or individual preference.

Fourth, *critical reflection* is not incompatible with *religious commitment*. The centre of religion is worship – not the acceptance of an interpretive hypothesis but the acknowledgment of that which is worthy of devotion. The necessity of personal involvement and the limitations of metaphysical speculation have been repeatedly emphasized. But these distinctive characteristics of religion need not exclude an attitude of self-critical questioning in the search for a truth beyond individual preference. As with the scientist, a commitment to honesty in the pursuit of truth is prior to commitment to a particular paradigm.

8

The Christian Paradigm

———

IN THIS CHAPTER some of the specific characteristics of the Christian paradigm are briefly explored. I will indicate some distinctive features of the Christian tradition and its understanding of its determinative exemplar, Jesus Christ. I will then discuss several models of God which have been employed, particularly two which have recently been developed under the influence of philosophical thought: the agent model and the process model. These remarks are intended only as illustrations of the methodological position of earlier chapters; a substantive account of models in the Christian tradition would require another volume.

1. THE HISTORICAL TRADITION

There can be complementary models within a paradigm, but paradigms are evidently not complementary; a person can fully share the outlook of only one tradition at a time. Religion, we have seen, is a way of life and not just a set of beliefs; it is an organic whole of which ideas are only one part. In becoming a member of a particular scientific or religious community, a person acknowledges its exemplars and comes to adopt its assumptions and expectations. Neither science nor religion is an individual enterprise; a person interprets his experience within a communal tradition. The concept of paradigm keeps before us the importance of a community of shared purposes, attitudes and presuppositions.

Participation in *a corporate history* is a striking feature of the practices of both Judaism and Christianity. Many aspects of congregational worship throughout the year are historical commemorations which portray the present life of individual and group in the light of the past. These communities are constituted not by isolated visions or mystical moments, but by a common life in response to historical events. God is identified not by metaphysical attributes but by historical relationships; he is 'the God of Abraham', 'the Lord who delivered us from bondage in Egypt', and 'the God and Father of our Lord Jesus Christ'. The chief forms of confession and creed are the recital of events rather than of general principles.

The *covenant at Sinai* is the central event in Israel's memory. The formation of a people, 'a holy nation', was important because only a community could adopt a life of obedience and justice. The covenant is a living relationship in every present, the enduring centre of the covenant community. Even the intense religious experience of individual prophets was always related to the ongoing life of the community. A recall to the covenant was a recall to the distinctive features of ethical monotheism: a God with moral purposes in history, who takes the initiative in judging and redeeming the life of a people and who is concerned with the total life of man because his purposes can be fulfilled only in the fabric of corporate life. Within this continuing community were particular individuals who served as exemplars in subsequent recollection: Abraham, Moses, David, the great prophets, priests and rabbis. Israel's memory of these exemplars has continued to preserve her distinctive religious beliefs.

The centre of the memory of *the Christian community* is of course the person of Christ. The disciples came to see Christ as both the fulfilment and the transformation of Israel's expectations. Here, too, it was through response to events in history, not to theological ideas, that the community came into being, and recollection of these events serves to preserve its distinctive beliefs. Once again, God was understood to be at work not simply in the lives of individuals but in the life of a group; the Holy Spirit was God's activity in the church, not in solitary religious experience. So great was the sense of mutual participation, and the dependence of each person on the life of the whole, that Paul could compare the church to a single organism (I Cor. 12.14). The church as a living community of forgiveness, mutual support and common memory is always the context of Christian life and thought.

But a tradition is *dynamic* and *developing*, not an unchanging legacy from the past. Like a living organism, it is historically continuous and yet always growing. A community can understand its exemplars and its historic origins in new ways and can adapt to new circumstances and new problems. There can thus be both diversity and novelty within a tradition as each generation looks at the present and the future in the light of the past. In modern times all the major religious traditions have gone through changes of unprecedented magnitude. As compared to scientific communities, religious communities are more dominated by the past and more reluctant to accept new ideas, but once again these are differences of degree rather than sharp contrasts.

In earlier chapters I have spoken of *the interpretation of experience*. Metaphors, I said, may momentarily encourage us to see patterns which we might not have noticed (the process which Black termed 'construing as'), but models systematically suggest distinctive ways of looking at things (for which I proposed the term 'interpreting as' in preference to Hick's phrase, 'experiencing as'). In using religious models we find new patterns in the world around us and in our lives. We interpret the world as a creation, and view our individual and corporate lives as a continuing dialogue with the divine Thou. Moral choice is understood as responsibility to both God and neighbour. A given community can use a variety of models in such interpretation, but its paradigm tradition sets limits on the range of acceptable models and gives emphasis to those experiences whose interpretation it considers most significant.

Within the Christian tradition, most of the types of experience which I have mentioned can be found in each historical period. Mystical awareness and numinous encounter can be illustrated from the writings of almost any century. One could cite a variety of examples in which there is reference to awe and reverence, moral obligation, interpersonal relationships, or order and creativity. But the experience of *reorientation and reconciliation* is perhaps most distinctive. Paul Tillich calls it 'the transition from estrangement to reconciliation'.[1] Our existence is estranged – from our true selves, from other persons, from the ground of meaning. But reconciliation with our true selves is possible: self-acceptance, liberation from bondage to self-concern, and internal integration in place of conflict and division. So also reconciliation with other people can occur: acceptance of others in sensitivity and forgiveness, a new freedom in interpersonal relationships, an openness to new possibilities of authentic human existence. Healing, wholeness, and renewal take place between persons and in communities of acceptance. This is experienced fulfilment and grace.

In such occurrences the *reconciling power of love* is at work. For a man to accept others he must know that he is accepted in a context wider than himself. Resources of healing and renewal must be grounded in the nature of the universe itself. The unforgiven is unable to forgive. In biblical terms, we can accept ourselves because God accepts us as we are; in the security of this relationship we are free to look at ourselves more honestly, released from guilt and self-hatred as well as from pride and self-righteousness. When a person is liberated from excessive self-concern and anxiety about his own status, he can forget about himself for a while and see the redemptive possibilities of reconciliation between man and man. These are the experiential dimensions of sin and salvation. For the Christian community such reorientation has occurred primarily through confrontation with the life of Christ. In that confrontation, renewal can be found, and at least in a fragmentary way, the power of reconciliation overcoming alienation, the healing of brokenness, the experience of release from guilt, anxiety and despair. In Christ's life were revealed new possibilities for authentic human existence in freedom, love and openness.

Let us consider Christ, then, as *exemplar* in the Christian paradigm. Eliade has said that the stories of most religious traditions narrate actions in primordial or historic time which serve as 'exemplars for emulation in the present'. As noted in Chapter 2, significant archetypal or historical events are understood to manifest the enduring structures of the cosmic order. Not an abstract ideal but a prototype for man's imitation is provided, along with exemplary patterns for ritual, moral and practical behaviour. Christ could be considered first as an exemplar in this sense. His life provides an image of authentic human existence, a style of life, a norm of integrity and love, which shapes our own self-understanding and action.

A religious tradition, like a scientific tradition, is transmitted more by *the memory of its exemplars* than by a set of explicit principles. For the Christian community, many incidents in Christ's life and the picture of him as a person have been influential. (For a scientific community, by contrast, a narrower range of incidents – such as Newton's experiments and ideas in mechanics, apart from his personal life – serve to transmit the tradition.) But the person of Christ is central also because the community has come to know the power of reconciling love at work in his life and thereby in the present also. To the community, his life is revelatory; these particular events illuminate other events. To abandon this paradigm is to make a decision about the occurrence of revelation.

In the biblical view, *history* is the most significant medium through which God expresses himself. Knowledge of God through nature and through religious experience is not denied but is carried further by knowledge of him through history. Response to historical events brings concrete religious communities into being; the celebration of these events is a continuing source of corporate identity and personal renewal and an occasion of worship. For the community of Israel, the judgment and mercy of God are seen in the prophetic interpretation of the redemptive events of its history. For the Christian community, the life of Christ is the focal expression of God's nature as sacrificial love. Christ is more than an exemplar for human emulation or a manifestation of the cosmic order, and we must give explicit attention to some of the ways in which he has been understood.

2. CHRISTOLOGICAL MODELS

Consider first the proposal that there have been complementary models used in interpreting *the person of Christ*. William Austin asks whether *humanity* and *divinity* can be thought of as complementary models of Christ.[2] Each model limits the use of the other (e.g. from Christ's humanity we cannot make the inference of sinfulness, and from his divinity we cannot make the inference of omniscience). Historically, the presence of the model of divinity discouraged the adoptionist view of a purely human Christ, while the model of humanity discouraged the docetic view of a divine figure disguised as man but not really man. The church fathers also clearly rejected any 'compromise model' of Christ as an angelic or quasi-divine being, intermediate in status between God and man. The Chalcedonian 'two natures' formula prevented either model from being developed in a way which would exclude the other one, and yet no unified model was advanced.

But Austin raises a number of objections to the idea of considering *divinity* and *humanity* as complementary models of Christ. Our ideas of God and man may not be 'clear, coherent, and definite enough to serve as models'. Again, our ideas of divinity and humanity are themselves influenced by our confrontation with the person of Christ. I would raise another objection: in the previous chapter I urged that the term 'complementary' be restricted to models which, like wave and particle, are on the same logical level. Divinity and humanity do not seem to satisfy this condition.

Austin's proposal of *Messiah* and *Logos* as complementary christological models more nearly satisfies these conditions.[3] Since both models combine divinity and humanity – though in differing ways – they are on essentially the same logical level. In the Old Testament, a Messiah was expected who would be a particular individual anointed by God to bring his Kingdom to fruition. This emphasis was carried on in the theology of Antioch, which insisted on Christ's full manhood in body, mind and soul. The Alexandrian school, on the other hand, viewed him primarily as the incarnation of the Logos, which is at once the universal divine principle, the cosmic structure and the eternal word. Austin shows that the Council of Chalcedon tried to affirm both these models without jeopardizing the unity of the person of Christ, and there may be at least a few parallels which can be drawn with complementarity in physics.

An interesting study of *christological models* has been written by John McIntyre.[4] The 'two-natures model' (which he takes as a single complex model involving both divine and human natures) has dominated Christian thought, but it has a number of limitations; it is tied to the Aristotelian categories of substance and attribute, and it tends to view the incarnation as the assumption of an abstract human nature rather than the personal individuality of a particular man. McIntyre holds that the 'psychological model' avoids these dangers and has been explored in the light of modern insights concerning selfhood; but it has usually ended with a merely human Christ. The 'revelation model' helps to restore the balance, using the dynamic categories of divine and human activity in place of the more static categories of substances and natures.

We are here concerned about McIntyre's methodology rather than the details of the three models he presents. He concludes that we should use them essentially *independently* of each other. He advises us not to mix models and not to transfer assumptions or categories from one to another. 'The recognition of the relative independence of the models from one another is one condition of greater variety in christological expression.'[5] In particular, the traditional 'two-natures model' should not be used as the norm for judging either the 'psychological model' of Christ's selfhood or the 'revelation model' of Christ's life revealing God to us. The future of each of these models 'rests in the expansion of its own possibilities'. McIntyre's thesis of the independence of models is indebted to Ian Ramsey's writings, which he cites at length. I have maintained that there is a greater degree of interaction and mutual limitation between models than what Ramsey presents. Christological models, in short, are not independent of each other, even when they are not unified into a single model.

I am in agreement, however, with many of McIntyre's remarks concerning the *functions* and *status* of christological models. He mentions their power in evoking commitment, trust and devotion; but he also points to their integrative function in co-ordinating beliefs, e.g., about ethics, the church and the world. He insists that models of Christ are interpretations of an historical figure, but he recognizes that there are no bare historical events devoid of interpretation. Again, the existential response of faith and obedience is a given in experience, but it is, likewise, by no means uninterpreted.[6] Yet he does not claim the security of models directly revealed to us but acknowledges them as 'partial insights':

> Whence do models derive? The answer that commends itself to my judgment is that the creation of models is part of the function which imagination fulfills in theological activity. . . . If models are deliverances of imagination, we shall be reluctant to claim for them immediately the sanctions of faith. They do not come to us with the authority of Christ himself.[7]

McIntyre outlines briefly several criteria for the evaluation of a christological model. (1) It 'correlates a higher proportion of the biblical material concerning Christ and of the church's witness to him'. (2) It sets these events in the widest possible context. (3) It 'throws light on the areas of our religious thought and action' and also 'illumines areas to which it was not in the first place directed'. (4) It 'leads to fresh commitment to Christ', mediates forgiveness and renewal, and calls forth 'our obedient and loving response'.[8]

A variety of analogies have been used to express the significance of *Christ's death*. These images of the atonement seem to have been used in a more sustained fashion than metaphors, though perhaps they are not developed systematically enough to be called models. However, they have been so influential in the history of Christian thought, ever since Paul wrote *Romans*, that I will consider them briefly as complementary models of the atonement. First, the *penal substitute* model uses the images of a law court. The satisfaction of justice requires a penalty for our offences; Christ as substitute bears our punishment and we are acquitted. This view emphasizes the costliness of sin and the vindication of the moral order. For Anselm, who made extensive use of it, this model was based on a profound experience of guilt interpreted by means of legal analogies.[9] Second, the *sacrificial victim* model uses the images of the temple sacrifice. Christ as both priest and victim (as in the letter to the Hebrews) provides expiation for man's sin. But this is no propitiation of an angry God, since God himself has provided the means for man's restoration.

Third, the *liberator* model draws its analogy from the redemption of a slave or the ransom of a prisoner. Here the Christian experience of release from bondage to guilt, self and legalism is compared to deliverance from slavery or captivity. Christ is the one who redeems us from bondage. Fourth, the *moral example* model puts even greater stress on man's response to Christ's life and death. Whereas the first two models sometimes seem to represent a mechanical and juridical transaction, the latter two stress personal and ethical dimensions, and the subjective side of man's response as well as the objective side of God's initiative. Perhaps also they emphasize God's love more than his justice; at the cross, reconciliation overcomes alienation. If reconciliation is indeed the basic Christian experience, we would be justified in giving greater attention to the latter models (liberator and moral example) than the former (penal substitute and sacrificial victim).[10]

Now these models of Christ might be considered complementary. Their joint use might prevent exclusive emphasis on either God's love or his justice, for example. A model which portrays divine initiative would limit the use of a model which portrays human response, and vice versa. But any model of Christ which makes reference to an attribute of God will today provide a problematical starting-point, since ideas of God are themselves in doubt for many people. It may be more helpful, therefore, to turn the problem around and ask whether the person of Christ may not be taken as a model of God.

3. FOUR MODELS OF GOD

We shall now turn to some models of God which have been used in the Christian tradition. In this section I will mention (1) monarchial, (2) deistic, (3) dialogic and (4) agent models. God's relation to the world is successively viewed as analogous to the relation between (1) a king and his kingdom, (2) a clockmaker and a clock, (3) one person and another person, and (4) an agent and his actions (or, in one version, a self and his body). In the subsequent section, a fifth model is presented, the social model of process philosophy, in which God's relation to the world is thought of as analogous to the relation between an individual and a community. At that point we will consider Christ as model of God. In accordance with the conclusions of Chapter 5 above, models consonant with the Christian paradigm are predominantly personal, but we will have to take into account the experiences which have led to impersonal models.

We have seen that the Bible used a variety of personal metaphors and images for God as Shepherd, Husband, Father, Judge, King, etc. The *monarchial model* of God as King was developed systematically, both in Jewish thought (God as Lord and King of the Universe), in medieval Christian thought (with its emphasis on divine omnipotence) and in the Reformation (especially in Calvin's insistence on God's sovereignty). In the portrayal of God's relation to the world, the dominant western historical model has been that of the absolute monarch ruling over his kingdom.

The biblical story of God's mighty acts was elaborated into the classical doctrine of *divine omnipotence*. God, it was said, governs and rules the world in his providential wisdom. He is free to carry out his purposes; all events are totally subordinate to his will. Divine foreordination was said to involve not only foreknowledge but also predetermination of every event. Both medieval Thomism and Reformation Protestantism held that God intervenes as a direct cause of particular events, in addition to his more usual action working through secondary natural causes. There is a strictly asymmetrical, one-way relation: God affects the world, but the world does not affect a God who is eternal, unchanging and impassible.

The monarchial model can be criticized for failing to allow adequately for *human freedom*. Predestination is incompatible with the existence of genuine alternatives in human choice; no subtleties in distinguishing foreknowledge from foreordination seem to be able to circumvent this basic contradiction. Man's total dependence on and submission to an authoritarian God is also in tension with human responsibility and maturity; supernaturalism has too often resulted in the repression rather than the fulfilment of man's natural vitalities. A further objection to the monarchial model is that it makes God responsible for *evil and suffering*. If all events are foreordained by God, is he not, inescapably, the author of evil? Finally, the doctrine of divine omnipotence runs counter to the idea of the *lawfulness of nature* which arose with the development of the scientific outlook.

With the growth of modern science in the seventeenth century, nature was increasingly viewed as a law-abiding machine. God was *the divine clockmaker* and the world was the clock – an autonomous and self-sufficient mechanism. Newton's contemporary, Robert Boyle, started by defending God's freedom and sovereignty but ended by asserting that God in his wisdom has planned things so that he does not have to intervene. The unfailing rule of law, not miraculous intervention, is the evidence of his benevolence. Providence is expressed not by his action in particular events but by the total cosmic design, the over-all structure and order of the world. This was the inactive God of Deism, who started the mechanism and then let it run by itself. Nature was viewed as a self-contained system whose interactions are to be exhaustively accounted for in the purely natural terms of lawful cause-and-effect. By the eighteenth century, the prevalent model of God's relation to nature was the clockmaker and the clock.

The third or *dialogic* model expresses the person-to-person character of God's relation to man. This interpersonal model was present in biblical writings, especially in the image of God as Father, but was recovered in recent centuries, partly in response to the impersonal character of God's relation to the world in Deism. The Methodist movement and later revivalism witnessed to the experience of reconciliation understood as person-to-person judgment, forgiveness and love. More recently, existentialist writers have depicted the dialogic character of the I-Thou encounter, the interaction of God and man in the present moment. The freedom of man, which was jeopardized in both the monarchial and deistic models, is here strongly defended.

But the dialogic model makes a sharper separation of *man* and *nature* than can be justified today. Evolutionary biology and ecology have shown us the continuities between the human and subhuman worlds. The existentialist dichotomy between the sphere of personal selfhood and the sphere of impersonal objects can be criticized equally on biblical grounds. The retreat to the realm of man's inwardness leaves nature unrelated to God and devoid of enduring significance. The world becomes the impersonal stage for the drama of human life, if not an object to be exploited for man's benefit. In the biblical view, by contrast, the natural world is no mere setting but part of the drama which is a single unified creative-redemptive work. Today we need a theology of nature as well as of human existence.

The fourth model, which I wish to discuss at greater length, does allow us to speak of God's relation to nature, yet without the coercive or mechanical implications of the monarchial and deistic models. This is the *agent* model which has been developed under the influence of recent work in linguistic philosophy. To understand it, one must start from an analysis of language about human agents and their actions. An *action* is a succession of activities ordered towards an end. Its unity consists in an intention to realize a goal. An action differs from a bodily movement. A given bodily movement (for example, moving my arm outward in a particular way) may represent a variety of actions (such as mailing a letter, sowing seeds, or dealing cards). Conversely, a given action may be carried out through a variety of sequences of bodily movements. An action cannot be specified, then, by any set of bodily movements, but only by its purpose or intent.[11]

Analysis in terms of *intentions* does not preclude analysis in terms of scientific laws. The physiologist need not refer to my purposes when he explains my arm movement. In addition, intentions are never directly observable. An action may be difficult to identify without a larger context. Calling it an action involves an interpretation of its meaning and often requires observation over a considerable temporal span; it may, of course, be misinterpreted and wrongly identified. The unity is one of intentionality rather than of causality. The agent of an action is an embodied subject acting through, not on, his body. Instead of a mind-body dualism of two distinct substances, we have two ways of talking about a single set of events. An agent is his living body in action, not an invisible mind interacting with a visible body. Yet the agent transcends any single action and is never fully expressed in any series of actions.

Now human action may be taken as a model of *divine action*. If God's action is identified in terms of his intentions, the cosmic drama can be interpreted as an expression of the divine purpose. God is understood to act in and through the structure and movement of nature and history. Gordon Kaufman suggests that the whole course of evolutionary development can be considered as one all-encompassing action unified by God's intentions. Within this master action are various sub-actions – the emergence of life, the advent of man, the growth of culture, etc. – which are phases of a total action moving towards greater consciousness, freedom and community. Kaufman sees the history of Israel and the life of Christ as special sub-actions decisively expressing the divine intention.[12]

Divine intentions do not enter the scientific account of cosmic history any more than human intentions enter the physiological account of an arm movement. John Compton writes:

> We can distinguish the causal development of events from the meaning of these events viewed as God's action. Scientific analysis of physical nature and of human history has no more need of God as an explanatory factor than the physiologist needs my conscious intent to explain my bodily movements. Nor does God need to find a 'gap' in nature in order to act, any more than you or I need a similar interstice in our body chemistry. Each story has a complete cast of characters, without the need for interaction with the other story, but quite compatible with it. What happens is that the evolution of things is *seen* or *read*, in religious life – as my arm's movement is read in individual life – as part of an action, as an expression of divine purpose, in addition to its being viewed as a naturalistic process.[13]

Further, we can maintain that God is not fully expressed in historical action even as a human agent is not fully expressed in any sequence of actions.

The *intentions of an agent* are never directly observable and may be difficult to guess from events in a limited span of time. In the case of religion, a paradigm tradition provides a vision of a wider context within which the pattern is interpreted. There is indeed a strong biblical precedent for talking about God in terms of his intentions and purposes in history. And today the linguistic approach would encourage us to treat the language of divine action as an alternative to scientific language, not a competitor with it. It would provide a model of *God as agent*, stressing intentionality rather than causality. The relation of a human agent to his acts would be taken as an analogy for the relation of God to cosmic history.

But a major objection may be raised concerning this analogy. We can identify a human agent by his *body*, even if we distinguish actions from bodily movements. But how can we identify God? Kai Nielsen claims that we can have no idea of bodiless spirit, since we have found nothing like it in our experience.[14] Is some reference to the body required in the language of action? There are two possible answers.

One might argue that *no bodily reference* is required in talking about intentions. Robert King reminds us that we do not have to observe our own bodily behaviour to know our intentions. Even the intentions of another person, he insists, are not read off directly, but involve a context of interpretation and the agent's testimony, the revelation of his intentions in word and act. Furthermore, says King, bodily reference is not required in order to identify God. Bodily continuity helps us distinguish among human agents, but God is distinguished from other agents by the universal scope of his action and by the perfect freedom and love made known in Christ.[15]

The second alternative would be to look on *the world as God's body*. As Compton points out, our bodies do have a measure of independence and autonomy as self-regulating systems. There is a 'wisdom of the body', apart from our conscious intentions. Without reverting to a mind-body dualism, we could point to the occasions on which the body is not merely the passive instrument of the will. So, too, the world has a limited independence over against God. 'Not everything that occurs in nature is an act of God', says Compton, 'any more than everything that occurs in (or to) me is my act.' In Compton's view, God is not an absolutely controlling agent. 'He is, as we are, *in fact incomplete*, incomplete in knowledge of and control over natural bodily history.'[16] But Compton acknowledges that this model does not allow sufficiently for the independence of God and the world.

A number of other limitations in the analogy of *the world as God's body* can be listed. The world does not overtly display the degree of unity which a human body possesses. To be sure, the mystical tradition has testified to an underlying unity, and has sometimes referred to God as the world-soul; but usually mystics speak of an undifferentiated identity wherein distinctions are obliterated – which is very different from the organized integration of co-operatively interacting parts that characterizes the unity of a body. A body has an external environment, whereas all interactions would be internal to the cosmic organism. We have not created our bodies, whereas the biblical tradition has held that God created the world. But the most serious objection is that the agent model does not preserve the independence and freedom of creatures in the world. Even if God is not an absolutely controlling agent, his relation to evil in the world remains problematical. God's relation to other agents seems to require a social or interpersonal analogy in which a plurality of centres of initiative are present. The biblical model of Father, after all, allowed for the presence of many agents, rather than concentrating on the divine agent alone. We will see that in the process model more than one agent may influence a given event, so that both God's action and that of other agents can be represented.

4. THE PROCESS MODEL

Four models of God's relation to the world have been mentioned, patterned respectively after an absolute monarch and his kingdom, a clockmaker and a clock, a dialogue between two persons, and an agent and his actions. In the process thought of Alfred North White-head, a fifth model is presented: a *society* of which one member is pre-eminent but not absolute. The universe is pictured as a community of interacting beings, rather than as a monarchy, a machine, an interpersonal dialogue or a cosmic organism.[17]

The process view of reality is *social* in that a plurality of centres of activity is envisaged. It could also be called *ecological* in that it starts from a network of relationships between interdependent beings, rather than from separate beings or dialogic pairs. Neither God nor man can be considered in isolation from the total process. Instead of the one-way action of God on the world, there is reciprocal interaction; giving and receiving, God and the world affect each other. The God of process thought is not immutable and independent, but changing and never completed, even though his essential nature does not change. Temporality and becoming characterize all participants in the community of being.[18]

Between God and the world there is *interdependence* and *reciprocity*, in the process view, but the relationship is not fully symmetrical. God is affected by the world, but he alone is everlasting and does not perish. God is not self-sufficient or impassible, for he is involved in time and history, but he is not totally within the temporal order. Events make a difference to him, but his purposes are unchanging. Divine immanence is thus more strongly emphasized than transcendence, yet God's freedom and relative independence are defended, along with his priority in status (though not priority in time). For nothing comes into being apart from God. Within the cosmic community, God has a unique and direct relationship to each member.

God's power is *the power of persuasion* rather than of coercion, of love rather than of compulsion. It is the lure of ideals which must be actualized by other beings. Whitehead rejects the image of God as the omnipotent monarch, the imperial ruler, in favour of what he calls 'the Galilean vision of humility', the idea of God as 'the fellow-sufferer who understands'.[19] God is like a wise parent whose educational influence on a growing child occurs through the love and respect he elicits and the ideals he holds up to the child. The power of love is its ability to evoke a response while respecting the integrity of the other.

In the Whiteheadian scheme every entity must *respond for itself*, and nothing that happens is God's act alone. God does not act directly but rather influences the creatures to act. Each entity has considerable independence and its response is genuinely its own. Process thinkers reject both omnipotence and predestination. If there is genuine freedom and novelty in the world, then even God cannot know the future until decisions have been made by individual agents. Time is not the unrolling of a scroll on which everything is already recorded; alternative possibilities are open until choices are made at many centres of responsibility. God interacts with the world in time, rather than determining it in his eternal decree. He respects the freedom of his creatures.

Whitehead's social model of reality is developed in a detailed *metaphysical system*; I can comment here on only a few features relevant to our discussion. He uses a set of very general categories which with suitable modifications can be applied to all kinds of entity. He thinks of every entity as a series of events, each of which is to be considered as a *moment of experience* that takes account of other events and responds to them. Causality, in Whiteheadian thought, is a complex process in which three strands are interwoven. Every new event is in part the product of efficient causation, that is, the influence of previous occurrences upon it. There is also an element of self-causation or self-creation, since every event unifies what is given to it by the past in its own manner from its unique perspective on the world. It contributes something of its own in the way it appropriates its past, relates itself to various possibilities, and produces a novel synthesis that is not strictly deducible from its antecedents. There is a creative selection from among alternative potentialities in terms of goals and aims, which is final causation. Every new occurrence can, in short, be looked on as a present response to past events in terms of potentialities grasped.

Now Whitehead ascribes the ordering of these potentialities to God. God as the *primordial ground of order* structures the potential forms of relationship before they are actualized. In this function God seems to be an abstract and impersonal metaphysical principle. But Whitehead's God also has specific purposes for the realization of maximum value. He selects particular possibilities for particular entities. He is *the ground of novelty* as well as of order. He presents new possibilities, among which there are alternatives left open. He elicits the self-creation of individual entities and thereby allows for freedom as well as structure. By valuing particular potentialities to which creatures respond, God influences the world without determining it. God acts by being experienced by the world, affecting the development of successive moments, participating in the unfolding of every event. But he never determines the outcome of events or violates the self-creation of each being. Every event is the joint product of past causes, divine purposes, and the emerging entity's own activity.

For Whitehead, God's action is *the evocation of response*. Since man's capacity for response far exceeds that of other beings, it is in human life that God's influence can be most effective. God's ability to engender creative change in lower beings seems to be very limited. He is always one factor among many, and particularly with respect to low-level beings, in which experience is rudimentary and creativity is minimal, his power seems to be negligible. Insofar as natural agents exercise causal efficacy, God's ability to compel change is thereby restricted. But we must remember that God is not absent from events that monotonously repeat their past, for he is the ground of order. At low levels, God's novel action may be beyond detection, though perhaps in cosmic history and emergent evolution there are signs of his creativity in the inanimate. Even when God does contribute to novelty he always acts along with other causes. We can never extricate the 'acts of God' from their involvement in the complex of processes through which he works. The Whiteheadian model thus leads to a metaphysical analysis which allows for the actions of a multiplicity of agents.

Charles Hartshorne follows Whitehead closely in his social model of reality but portrays a greater unity in the cosmic process. He holds that the world is in God (*panentheism*), a view which neither identifies God with the world (pantheism) nor separates him from it (theism). 'God includes the world, but is more than the world.'[20] Hartshorne is willing to say that 'the world is in a sense the body of God'.[21] We are cells in the divine organism. The world-soul is immanent in the dynamic unity of the world, as man's mind is immanent in his body. This view gives less scope than Whitehead's does for the integrity and freedom of a plurality of individual agents. The objections to the analogy of the world as God's body, advanced in the preceding section, seem to hold even if we grant that a cell in the body has considerable independence and 'a life of its own'.

John Cobb, on the other hand, thinks that it would be compatible with Whiteheadian thought to speak of God as a '*person*' in interaction with other beings. Whitehead himself ascribes personal qualities to God (consciousness, purpose, freedom, and creativity); his God is by no means an impersonal principle, as some of his critics have claimed. But Whitehead does refrain from calling God a 'person', which he thinks of as a succession of moments of experience with a special continuity. He allows for real becoming in God, and yet wants to treat God's existence throughout time as a single occasion, since it involves complete self-identity and no loss of what is past. Cobb argues that it would be consistent with Whitehead's own understanding of God's becoming, as well as with the biblical tradition, to consider God a 'living person', an infinite succession of occasions.[22] God would be the pre-eminent person in a community of interacting beings. Cobb's writings develop the pluralism and personalism of the process model.

5. MODELS, PARADIGMS AND METAPHYSICS

In previous chapters it has been suggested that the basic assumptions of a paradigm community influence its choice of models. It has been shown that models have important non-cognitive functions, especially in the expression and evocation of attitudes. In addition, it has been argued that models lead to beliefs which can be evaluated by criteria that are at least partially independent of particular paradigms, including simplicity, conformity to experience, coherence and comprehensiveness. I can indicate in only the briefest way how these considerations might be applied to the five models discussed above.

The priority of the *monarchial* model seems to be supported by the centrality of numinous experience and worship in the Christian tradition. But serious questions can be raised as to whether the doctrine of omnipotence to which it has led is compatible with the example of Christ the exemplar, on the one hand, or with human experience, especially with regard to human freedom and the existence of evil, on the other. The *dialogic* model does not encounter these difficulties, and is particularly suitable for interpreting the Christian experience of reconciliation overcoming estrangement, and the more personal dimensions of guilt and forgiveness. But neither the monarchial nor the dialogic model illuminates the relation of God and man to nature as understood by modern science, which a sufficiently comprehensive model must take into account.

It is in relating God to nature that the *deistic* and *agent* models purport to be most helpful. But the mechanistic view of nature in deism can itself be challenged, as we will see, from the standpoint of post-Newtonian science. The clockmaker God, who leaves the world-machine to run on its own, is neither an object of worship nor a participant in human experience, and bears little resemblance to the God of the Bible. The agent model is closer to the biblical tradition when it identifies God by his actions and intentions. The language of intentions need not conflict with the language of scientific law in describing either human or divine action. But most expositions of the agent model offer the analogy of the world as God's body, which seems to jeopardize the independence of other agents and the freedom of man.

It appears that the strength of the *dialogic* model lies in its ability to depict God's relation to man, whereas the *agent* model is most valuable in depicting God's relation to nature. It might be proposed that these two models should be treated as complementary; the strengths of one seem to be precisely the weaknesses of the other. But I will propose instead that, if the *process* model is given priority, then nature, man and God can all be coherently represented; the other models would then serve secondary roles in thinking about particular interactions within the more inclusive process model.

I have maintained that one of the principal functions of religious language is the interpretation of *religious experience* and *corporate history*. The context of religious discourse is the worshipping community. Writings in process philosophy, by contrast, seem abstract and speculative. The God of metaphysics seems to serve quite different functions from the God of worship. He is described in philosophical and ontological categories, rather than the historical and personal categories of the Bible. But this criticism is less impressive if we look at the *theological use* of these philosophical categories in the interpretation of the experiences which the paradigm community considers most significant. I submit that the idea of a God of persuasion is particularly appropriate to the experience of reconciliation and to the historical person of Christ.

A number of authors have made use of process categories in the expression of *Christian theology*.[23] The process model leads to an emphasis on certain biblical themes which were minimized in later Christian thought, such as God's participation in temporal process and the vulnerability of suffering love. Process theology abandons the model of the absolute monarch but retains a personal model of God and his role in the cosmic society. In the last analysis, the most central Christian model for God is not a king or a clockmaker but the person of Christ himself. In that person it is love, even more than justice or power, which is manifest. Process theology reiterates on a cosmic scale the motif of the cross, the power of a love which accepts suffering.

To the Christian community, then, Christ is more than a historical exemplar; he is a model for God. But process thought, by envisaging the Christ-model within the larger model of the cosmic society, can preserve a number of features of the other models expounded above. In portraying God's relationship to man, the interpersonal character of the dialogic model can be retained, without neglecting other beings or the social context within which such dialogue occurs. In portraying God's relationship to nature, there is represented both the interdependence of all beings and their significant independence, which the agent model tends to compromise.

But could one *worship* the God of process theology? In a widely reprinted essay, J. N. Findlay claimed that only a necessary being is a fitting object of worship.[24] In a recent book, H. P. Owen contends that worship, adoration and self-commitment can only be given to a God who is self-existent and 'sovereign over all that exists'. 'We cannot validly commit ourselves without reservation to

God's loving providence unless all things are completely subject to his power'.[25] In reply, one might cite an article in which Peter Appleby concludes that the religious attitudes of trust, love, awe, gratitude and repentance presuppose a personal deity, but not a necessary or omnipotent being.[26] Process theologians have held that it is God's goodness, not his power, which justifies reverence and worship, though presumably a totally impotent deity would evoke pity more than respect. In any case, the process God, though not omnipotent, is not dependent on the world as the world is dependent on him; his ideal purposes are not contingent on events in the world. Every being is indebted to God for its existence as well as for the order of possibilities it can actualize. In Whitehead's words, 'God is not before all creation but with all creation.' Such a God is surely worthy of worship.

Next, it should not be overlooked that any model of God's relation to nature reflects a particular *view of nature*. In the Newtonian view, which prevailed until the last century, nature was essentially static, with all things presumed to have been created in their present forms. Nature was deterministic, its future in principle predictable from knowledge of the present. The model of clock and clockmaker seemed entirely appropriate. But today nature is seen as a dynamic process of becoming, always changing and developing, radically temporal in character; this is an incomplete cosmos still coming into being. Nature is unpredictable, especially at the level of quantum physics; the billiard-ball model is outdated. Evolution is a creative process whose outcome is not predictable. It is just this combination of order and creativity which process thought seeks to interpret. Considerable scientific evidence supporting the unity of man and nature could also be adduced.

Process thought provides distinctive analyses of the problems of *freedom* and *evil*. The ways in which freedom is built into process metaphysics from the outset have already been indicated. If the classical ideas of omnipotence and predestination are given up, God is exonerated of responsibility for natural evil. If no event is the product of God's agency alone, he works with a world, given to him in every moment, which never fully embodies his will. The creatures, and above all man, are free to reject the higher vision. Suffering is inevitable in a world of beings with conflicting goals. Pain is part of the price of consciousness and intensity of feeling. In an evolutionary world, struggle is integral to the realization of greater value. As Teilhard de Chardin maintained, evil is intrinsic to an evolving cosmos as it would not be to an instantaneous creation. Suffering and death are not punishments for sin but structural concomitants of what he called 'the immense travail' of a world in birth.[27]

The *ethical implications* of process thought should also be considered if indeed the evocation of attitudes is an important function of religious language. Process theology pictures a teleological universe in which love is central and man has an important role. Too often in the past we have viewed God as the authoritarian judge, the represser of human vitalities. Process thought sees him as the fulfiller of man, calling forth our capacities for a more fully human existence. Our own responsibility is enhanced if we believe that God does nothing by himself. We are co-creators in an unfinished universe, participants in God's continuing work. God calls us to love, freedom and justice. Time, history and nature are to be affirmed, for it is here that God's everlasting purposes can be carried forward.

We may observe also that process thought encourages *attitudes towards nature* conducive to ecological awareness. It stresses the interdependence of man and nature, instead of treating nature as an object alien to man. Its theme of divine immanence would engender respect for the natural world. Process thinkers have offered a theology of nature – a topic sadly neglected in neo-orthodoxy, existentialism, and most other twentieth-century schools of Christian thought – and it would strongly support an environmental ethic.[28]

Finally, an evaluation of process theology would have to assess the wider system of *process metaphysics* according to the criteria presented in Chapter 7 above. It could be shown to rate highly in coherence (internal consistency and systematic interrelatedness) and comprehensiveness (the ordering of diverse types of experience). Does it adequately represent the diversity of experience? I have said that metaphysical systems tend to distort the pluralism and variety of experience; in the interests of coherence and comprehensiveness they tend to impose a set of categories from one domain as the key to the interpretation of all domains. Fidelity to experience, I have urged, comes before simplicity and comprehensiveness. In particular, the 'panpsychist' theme in process thought can be criticized for failing to distinguish sufficiently between animate and inanimate beings. It should be noted, however, that Whitehead does allow great diversity in the ways in which his fundamental categories are applied to different levels of being; he does not, for instance, ascribe consciousness to lower-level organisms, much less to inanimate objects. With regard to the higher levels, it may be questioned whether Whitehead's account of the continuity and identity of the human self is satisfactory.

I have maintained that *the use of metaphysical categories* in theology is inescapable, but that the theologian should be cautious about identifying religious beliefs with any closed metaphysical system. All theologians use metaphysical categories, especially in discussing God's relation to nature; Augustine was indebted to Plato, Aquinas to Aristotle, Barth to Kant (despite his disclaimers). Christianity cannot be equated with any particular philosophical synthesis, and the absolute claims for a metaphysical system which characterized medieval Christendom should be avoided. The theologian must adapt, not adopt, a metaphysics; many of the process insights can be accepted without accepting the total Whiteheadian scheme. These insights can lead to the modification of classical religious models so that they more accurately reflect the experience of the Christian community. I hope to explore these substantive questions in another volume. In this chapter I have referred to them only as an illustration of relationships between models, paradigms, and experience.

9

Conclusions

IN THIS CHAPTER I will summarize briefly the conclusions to which the reflections of this volume seem to point and then indicate some implications for the study of religion, attitudes towards other religions and personal religious faith.

Many philosophers in the last two decades, under the influence of writings in the philosophy of science which extolled the objectivity of science, were led to assert that religion can make no legitimate *cognitive claims*. Accepting an oversimplified view of science as the prototype for all genuine knowledge, they concluded that religious language serves only non-cognitive functions. I have suggested, however, that science is not as objective, nor religion as subjective, as the view dominant among philosophers of religion has held. Man the knower plays a crucial role throughout science. Scientific models are products of creative analogical imagination. Data are theory-laden; comprehensive theories are resistant to falsification; and there are no rules for paradigm choice. To be sure, each of these subjective features is more prominent in religion; there is a greater diversity of models, greater influence of interpretation on data, greater tenacity in commitment to paradigms, and greater ambiguity in paradigm choice. But in each of these features I see a difference of degree between science and religion rather than an absolute contrast. These comparisons can be made without denying the distinctive non-cognitive functions of religious language which have no parallel in science.

In particular, I have tried to show that the demand of some

philosophers for the specification of *falsifying conditions* for religious beliefs is unreasonable. Flew's challenge, which set the terms for the falsification debate during the 1960's, is not a reasonable one if it cannot be met by comprehensive scientific theories. Flew assumed that there are two mutually exclusive classes of statements, 'falsifiable' and 'unfalsifiable'. Instead, I have portrayed a spectrum of degrees of resistance to falsification. Though no decisive falsification is possible in religion, I have argued that the cumulative weight of evidence does count for or against religious beliefs. Religious paradigms, like scientific ones, are not falsified by data, but are replaced by promising alternatives. Commitment to a paradigm allows its potentialities to be systematically explored, but it does not exclude reflective evaluation.

In discussing both models and paradigms I have defended *critical realism*. I have tried to show that, among the wide variety of kinds of models, there are some which are neither literal pictures of reality (naive realism) nor useful fictions (instrumentalism). I have also indicated that the occurrence of major paradigm shifts, rather than simple cumulation or convergence in the history of science, militates against naive realism. The dominance of paradigms in the life and thought of a religious community is even stronger than that in a scientific community, and naive realism is correspondingly more difficult to accept. Yet acknowledgment of the influence of paradigms need not lead us to instrumentalism or a total relativism concerning truth-claims. For I have maintained that in both science and religion there are experiential data and criteria of judgment which are not totally paradigm-dependent, though I have granted that the absence of rules for choice among paradigms is far more problematic in religion than in science.

The critical realism which this view of models and paradigms supports has important implications for *the study of religion*. The teaching of religion in theological seminaries has often assumed a naive realism. Especially in traditional and orthodox circles, one true religion has been advocated and other traditions have been dismissed as false or relegated to a lower level of spiritual understanding.

At the opposite extreme, the study of religion in secular universities has in the past often been based on instrumentalist or functionalist assumptions. This has frequently led to a reductionism in which religion is taken to be entirely the product of psychological or sociological forces. But recent years have seen the growth of religion departments in which the categories of interpretation within religious communities are taken seriously but no tradition is treated as absolute.

Robert Bellah has given an interesting analysis of these three positions:

> For the religiously orthodox, religious belief systems were felt to represent 'objective' reality as it really is, and thus if one of them is true the others must be false, either absolutely or in some degree. For the secular orthodox, all religion is merely 'subjective', based on emotion, wish or faulty inference, and therefore false. For the third group, who take symbolism seriously, religion is seen as a system of symbols which is neither simply objective nor simply subjective, but which links subject and object in a way that transfigures reality or even, in a sense, creates reality. For people with this point of view the idea of finding more than one religion valid, even in a deeply personal sense, is not only possible but normal. This means neither syncretism nor relativism, since it is possible within any social or personal context to develop criteria for the evaluation of religious phenomena and a consequent hierarchy of choice.[1]

Bellah calls his own view '*symbolic realism*' and he contrasts it both with the 'primary naiveté' and 'objectivism' of orthodoxy, and with the 'functional reductionism' and 'subjectivism' common in the social sciences. Bellah maintains that reality resides not in the object or subject alone but in the relation between them. Symbols not only express the feelings and attitudes of subjects but 'organize and regulate the flow of interaction between subjects and objects'. Religion is a symbol system which serves to evoke 'the totality which includes subject and object and provides the context in which life and action finally have meaning'.[2]

The *phenomenology of religion* is a method of study which is particularly consonant with critical realism. The phenomenological approach was developed by continental scholars in the history of religions but is increasingly represented in English-speaking universities.[3] Four of its characteristic interests may be summarized as follows:

1. *The meaning of religion to its adherents.* Instead of reducing religion to something else by interpreting it in categories foreign to its participants, one should try to look at religion in its own terms. The scholar should imaginatively enter into the activities and ideas of the religious community and ask about its interest and outlook, the phenomena as they appear to the persons involved.

2. *The variety of religious phenomena.* Phenomenologists study myths and rituals as well as doctrines and ideas, systems of action as well as systems of belief. They are interested in the diversity of religious experience as much as in religious institutions and leadership roles. They try to see a religious community in the organic wholeness of its life, action and thought before generalizing about similarities between different traditions.

3. *Patterns common to diverse cultures.* The comparative study of many religious traditions reveals typical forms which recur frequently. For example, sacrifice, sacraments, or prayer each has a characteristic constellation of meanings despite cultural variations. The phenomenologist is interested in basic structures of consciousness, types of religious expression, forms of representation and institutional patterns. He attempts a careful comparison of structurally similar experiences, acts and forms of life, such as feelings of awe and peace, initiatory ceremonies and priesthood roles. He finds these forms in the 'primitive' religions of archaic civilizations and preliterate cultures today as well as in the 'higher' religions.

4. *The suspension of judgment.* The phenomenologist tries to be descriptive; he avoids passing judgment on the truth or falsity of the beliefs held by the persons he is studying. Philosophical questions are bracketed; theological claims are acknowledged as important to the believing community without being either accepted or rejected by the investigator. Attention is focused on the explanations given by the participants.

Phenomenology is compatible with a non-reductionist instrumentalism which is sensitive to the variety of functions of religious language. However, the *critical realism* to which the discussion of models and paradigms points offers several advantages. It gives stronger support to the phenomenologist's concern for the meaning of religion to its adherents, since it takes seriously their systems of belief. To be sure, the paradigms of the scholar's own community will influence his viewpoint. He can never completely enter the interpretive framework of a culture vastly different from his own. But he can so immerse himself in its life and thought that he can sympathetically imagine how the world would look from another perspective.

Critical realism would encourage a variety of ways of studying religion in addition to the phenomenological approach.[4] The contribution of *sociological* methods would be welcomed, since religion is indeed a social reality expressed in social institutions. In analysing paradigms, the importance of the religious community and the assumptions which dominate its life was underscored. Sociologists and anthropologists have investigated the social functions of religion in the unification of a community, the celebration of its shared values, the legitimation or criticism of its authority structures, and so forth. They have enquired about relationships between religious identification and economic class, political behaviour, ethical values, family stability, etc. All of these societal phenomena can be studied empirically by the social sciences, without the assumption that religion is entirely a product of social forces or that only social functions are significant.

Similarly, the importance of the *psychology of religion* can be acknowledged. Whatever else it may be, religion is a means of personal adjustment and self-fulfilment which has creative or destructive effects on human personality. Religious beliefs and attitudes are integrally related to a person's self-image and the way he integrates his experiences, values and goals. Guilt, anxiety, emotional development, religious conversion, peak experiences, and responses to death are among the phenomena in human life which can be analysed by the psychologist. Nor should we neglect the *historical* approach in which the development in time of a single tradition is studied. Here the focus is on the concrete particularities of unique situations – which the phenomenologist tends to neglect in his search for the universal forms and basic essence of religion. The impact of particular men and movements, the temporal changes in institutions and ideas, and the relationships between events in their wider cultural context are typical concerns of the historian.

But critical realism can also find room for studies in which the question of the truth and falsity of religious beliefs is not bracketed. The *philosophy of religion* can deal with the diverse functions of religious language, cognitive as well as non-cognitive, and with the grounds for belief, as I have proposed in earlier chapters. It can examine the presuppositions and the logic of classical arguments and their modern reformulations. The interests of language analysis, epistemology, metaphysics and ethics can all be brought to bear on the study of religion. Finally, *theology* need not be excluded, though under the aegis of critical realism it would be undertaken in a distinctive way, as I will indicate below. Theology is the systematic and self-critical reflection of a paradigm community concerning its beliefs. The theologian traces the ways in which the memory of historical exemplars has shaped the life and thought of the community. He explores the relationships among its central models and doctrines and the implications of its views of nature, man and God.

I shall suggest next some implications of this volume for *attitudes towards other religions* in a pluralistic world. The recognition that models are not pictures of reality can contribute to tolerance between religious communities. In a day when the religions of the world confront each other, the view offered here might engender humility and tentativeness in the claims made on behalf of any one model. In place of the absolutism of exclusive claims to finality, an ecumenical spirit would acknowledge a plurality of significant religious models, without lapsing into a complete relativism which would undercut all concern for truth. We must be sensitive to the experience of men in other cultures and the models they use to interpet their experience; we must avoid the theological imperialism to which preoccupation with doctrines, along with literalism in interpretation, have often led.

I have held that persons of diverse traditions can appeal to *aspects of experience* which they share and can discuss together their interpretive frameworks. Communication is possible and religious beliefs are not incommensurable. For the person who is open to how other people think and feel, encounter with members of other traditions can be an occasion for extending the range of experience, understanding a variety of ways of being human, and seeing new possibilities for realizing his own humanity to which he may have been blinded by the limitations of his culture. The ability to listen as well as to speak is a pre-requisite of genuine dialogue.

It is clear that I have taken issue with the *absolutism* of orthodoxy, which asserts that one religion is true and other religions are false. Such dogmatism and exclusivism have led to religious wars and crusades and more subtle forms of religious imperialism which can hardly be countenanced in a global society. But it should also be clear that I do not accept the *relativism* which has often replaced it. Cultural relativism has asserted that each religion can be considered only as a product of its culture. Personal relativism makes religion entirely a matter of individual preference, or of what is 'true for me'. There are no criteria beyond the culture, in the one case, or the individual in the other, by which religions can be evaluated. I have maintained, on the contrary, that religious beliefs are open to discussion, and grounds for preference can be given.

Nor is there an easy answer to religious pluralism in claims of *the basic identity of all religions*. There have been various attempts to show that all religions are really the same, or that there is a common essence or a central core beneath the multiplicity of external forms.[5] Deism sought a universal core of ideas (e.g. the fatherhood of God and the brotherhood of man). Romanticism sought a universal type of experience, such as mysticism. Still others looked for a universal quality of feeling, such as absolute dependence (Schleiermacher), power (van der Leeuw) or awe (Otto). The problem with this approach is that from the rich diversity within any tradition, or among traditions, one element has been selected for emphasis. Even the attempt to delineate two basic strands, the numinous and the mystical (Chapter 5 above), must not be construed as an exhaustive characterization, and must be coupled with recognition of the great differences between religious traditions.

The approach to other religions which I am advocating is the way of *dialogue*. It respects the integrity of other traditions and the presence of irreducible differences. Yet it seeks to understand and appreciate other ways of life from within. Humility and openness enable learning to occur where defensiveness only narrows one's outlook. For the Christian, this path involves the recognition that God has been at work in other religious traditions; their faith and thought may be genuine responses to God in the context of their cultural assumptions. We can affirm the presence of God in the life of another person. M. A. C. Warren, for many years the General Secretary of the Church Missionary Society of the Church of England, speaks eloquently of the need for:

> a deep humility, by which we remember that God has not left himself without a witness in any nation at any time. When we approach the man of another faith than our own it will be in a spirit of expectancy to find how God has been speaking to him and what new understandings of the grace and love of God we may ourselves discover in this encounter. Our first task in approaching another people, another culture, another religion, is to take off our shoes, for the place we are approaching is holy.[6]

Finally, what are the implications of these chapters for *personal religious faith*? One of our recurrent themes has been the *experiential basis* of religion, which is as essential for renewed religious vitality in practice as for a defensible epistemology in theory. Inherited models are for many individuals today almost totally detached from human life. The experiences which traditional models once interpreted are in large measure ignored or suppressed. For example, the experience of reverence and wonder is not nurtured by the technological mentality that looks on the world – and even on human beings – as objects to be controlled and manipulated. As man's ancient dependence on nature has been replaced by various forms of dominion and mastery, the destructive consequences of this arrogance have become increasingly evident in the despoilation of the environment. Hopefully a new recognition of interdependence and a new respect for nature may be ecologically beneficial and at the same time foster the sort of humility which is a pre-requisite for religious reverence.[7]

We need a greater awareness of the *experiential correlates* of theological concepts. Sin and salvation are theological abstractions for many persons today, but the power of reconciliation overcoming estrangement, to use Tillich's terminology, is still a reality in human existence. Thoughtful men and women are seeking ways to express this message in the context of the life situations in which they find themselves. There are new theological articulations arising from black awareness, from women's consciousness and from movements for social justice.[8] But the heart of the Christian gospel is still the experience of forgiveness, love and grace in personal life. Only when we are freed from excessive self-concern can we begin to forget about ourselves. The knowledge that we are accepted can release us from anxiety about our own status and enable us to be more open to others. The possibility held before us is a new freedom in human relationships and a greater capacity for genuine concern and sensitivity.

The idea of *models* in the interpretation of such experiences may answer some of the difficulties in talking about God which are now felt so widely. One need not have followed the falsification debate among philosophers to have had doubts about the intellectual respectability of belief in God. The problems in any literalistic understanding of religious language, which were identified long before the rise of science, have been more generally acknowledged in an age of science. I have proposed that the idea of models provides a new form of analogical thinking which is not dependent on the metaphysical assumptions of the scholastic doctrine of analogy. As model-building becomes increasingly common in many fields, 'thinking in models' may be a useful point of entry into theological reflection. The term 'myth', by contrast, is so generally assumed to mean simply 'an untrue story' that it is probably impossible for most people to take the cognitive functions of myth seriously.

A combination of *faith* and *doubt* in personal religious life is another implication of critical realism. The 'critical' element includes recognition of the limitations of religious models. Doubt challenges all dogmatisms and calls into question the neat schemes in which we think we have the truth all wrapped up. There is a 'holy insecurity', as Buber calls it, in our lack of certainty about the finality of our formulations. There is a risk in acting on the basis of any interpretive framework which is not subject to conclusive proof. Faith, then, does not mean intellectual certainty or the absence of doubt, but rather a trust and commitment even when there are no guaranteed beliefs or infallible dogmas. Faith takes us beyond a detached and speculative outlook into the sphere of personal involvement.

Even in science, I have maintained, *commitment* to a paradigm tradition and tenacity in sticking to a research programme are justifiable. The basic assumptions of the tradition are acquired less from formal principles than from familiarity with its historical exemplars; commitment to a scientific paradigm allows its potentialities to be systematically explored. In religion, commitment to a paradigm implicates a wider range of dimensions of human personality, since religion serves non-cognitive functions which have no equivalent in science. Religious language is inherently self-involving and evaluational. Religious models express and elicit ethical dedication and commitment to policies of action. The language of the religious community arises in worship and meditation; it manifests attitudes of contrition, praise and gratitude, as well as aspiration and hope. The experience of reconciliation and re-orientation affects many areas of human thought, emotion, and behaviour.

The conjunction of *commitment* and *enquiry* is not easily achieved. Religion is a way of life; its dominant interest is practical rather than theoretical. It demands existential involvement not unlike that required to understand another human being at the deepest level. The detached and analytic view of the observer may preclude the sorts of experience which are crucial to the participant. But I have urged that commitment does not rule out critical reflection, continued enquiry, and dedication to the search for a truth beyond individual preference. There are criteria which are not entirely paradigm-dependent: coherence, comprehensiveness, and consistency with experience. There is also self-criticism in the moral realm.

The prophetic voices in every tradition have not hesitated to denounce the attitudes and behaviour of their own religious community.

Theology today must be both *confessional* and *self-critical*. We can only say: this is what has happened to us and to others in our tradition, and this is how things look from where we stand in our paradigm community. Self-criticism arises from the admission that all our formulations are partial and limited, coupled with the conviction that there are criteria in terms of which religious beliefs can be assessed. Such an approach acknowledges the historical conditioning of every set of conceptual categories and the finitude of every human viewpoint, while insisting that even one's most fundamental beliefs can be analysed and discussed. Perhaps the new views of science described in this volume can offer some encouragement to such a combination of commitment and enquiry in religion.

NOTES

Chapter 2   SYMBOL AND MYTH

1. Max Black, *Models and Metaphors*, Cornell University Press 1962, chaps. 3 and 13.

2. See Douglas Berggren, 'The Use and Abuse of Metaphor', *Review of Metaphysics*, vol. 16, 1962, pp. 237 and 450.

3. Monroe Beardsley, 'Metaphor', in P. Edwards (ed.), *Encyclopedia of Philosophy*, Macmillan 1967; M. McCloskey, 'Metaphors', *Mind*, vol. 73 1964, p. 215; Martin Foss, *Symbol and Metaphor in Human Experience*, Princeton University Press 1949.

4. Philip Wheelwright, *Metaphor and Reality*, Indiana University Press 1962, p. 162; see also his *The Burning Fountain*, Indiana University Press 1954.

5. Edwyn Bevan, *Symbolism and Belief*, Allen & Unwin 1938.

6. Wheelwright, *Metaphor and Reality*, chap. 6.

7. Ian Ramsey, *Christian Discourse*, Oxford University Press 1965, chap. 2; F. W. Dillistone, *Christianity and Symbolism*, Collins 1955.

8. Paul Tillich, *Dynamics of Faith*, Allen & Unwin and Harper & Row 1957, chap. 3.

9. Peter Slater, 'Parables, Analogues and Symbols', *Religious Studies*, vol. 4, 1968, p. 27.

10. C. H. Dodd, *The Parables of the Kingdom*, Nisbet & Co. 1935, p. 16.

11. Joachim Jeremias, *The Parables of Jesus* trans. S. H. Hooke, SCM Press and Charles Scribner's Sons 1963, p. 105. See also Robert W. Funk, *Language, Hermeneutic and Word of God*, Harper & Row 1966, chap. 5.

12. H. H. Price, *Thinking and Experience*, Hutchinson's University Library 1953, chap. 8.

13. Austin Farrer, *The Glass of Vision*, Dacre Press 1948, chap. 3.

14. Battista Mondin, *The Principle of Analogy in Protestant and Catholic Thought*, The Hague: Martinus Nijhoff 1963; James Ross, 'Analogy as a Rule of Meaning for Religious Language', *International Philosophical Quarterly*, vol. 1, 1961, p. 468; E. L. Mascall, *Existence and Analogy*, Longmans Green 1949; George Klubertanz, *St Thomas Aquinas on Analogy*, Loyola University Press 1960.

15. Mircea Eliade, *Patterns in Comparative Religion* trans. R. Sheed, Sheed & Ward 1958; Peter Berger, *The Sacred Canopy*, Doubleday & Co. 1967; Frederick Streng, *Understanding Religious Man*, Dickenson 1969.

16. Mircea Eliade, *The Sacred and the Profane* trans. W. Trask, Harcourt, Brace & World 1959, chap. 2.

17. G. van der Leeuw, *Religion in Essence and Manifestation* trans. J. E. Turner, Allen & Unwin, 1938 chap. 60.

18. H. R. Willoughby, *Pagan Regeneration*, University of Chicago Press 1929; Joseph Campbell, *The Masks of God: Occidental Mythology*, Viking Press 1964; Arnold van Gennep, *The Rites of Passage*, Routledge & Kegan Paul 1963.

19. See chapters by Stanley Edgar Hyman and Lord Raglan in Thomas A. Seboek (ed.), *Myth: A Symposium*, University of Indiana Press 1958; also S. H. Hooke (ed.), *Myth and Ritual*, Oxford University Press 1933.

20. Clyde Klukhohn, 'Myth and Ritual: A General Theory', *Harvard Theological Review*, vol. 35, 1942, p. 45, reprinted in W. A. Lessa and E. Z. Vogt (eds), *Reader in Comparative Religion*, Harper & Row 1965.

21. See chapters by John F. Priest and Amos N. Wilder in Joseph Campbell (ed.), *Myths, Dreams and Religion*, E. P. Dutton & Co. 1970.

22. E.g., the essay by Alasdair MacIntyre in A. MacIntyre (ed.), *Metaphysical Beliefs*, SCM Press 1957; or Langdon Gilkey, *Religion and the Scientific Future*, Harper & Row 1970.

23. See J. F. M. Middleton (ed.), *Myth and Cosmos*, Doubleday and Co. 1967.

24. Sigmund Freud, *The Interpretation of Dreams* trans. J. Strachey, Modern Library and Basic Books 1955.

25. Claude Lévi-Strauss, *Structural Anthropology* trans. C. Jacobson and B. G. Schoepf, Basic Books 1963; Edmund Leach, *Lévi-Strauss*, Fontana 1970.

26. Alasdair MacIntyre, 'Myth', in P. Edwards (ed.), *Encyclopedia of Philosophy*, vol. 5, p. 435.

27. Annemarie de Waal Malefijt, *Religion and Culture*, Macmillan 1968, chap. 7.

28. Henry A. Murray, 'The Possible Nature of a "Mythology" to Come', in Henry A. Murray (ed.), *Myth and Mythmaking*, George A. Braziller, 1960.

29. Ernst Cassirer, *Language and Myth* trans. S. Langer, Peter Smith Publishers and Harper & Brothers 1946; *The Philosophy of Symbolic Forms*, vol. II, trans. R. Manheim, Yale University Press 1955.

30. C. G. Jung and C. Kerenyi, *Essays on a Science of Mythology* trans. R. F. C. Hull, Princeton University Press 1969; Maud Bodkin, *Studies in Type Images in Poetry, Religion and Philosophy*, Oxford University Press 1951; also Wheelwright (note 4 above).

31. Rudolf Bultmann, *Jesus Christ and Mythology*, Charles Scribner's Sons 1958.

Chapter 3   MODELS IN SCIENCE

1. An earlier version of Section I of this chapter appeared in Chapter 1 of

Ian G. Barbour, *Science and Secularity: The Ethics of Technology*, Harper & Row 1970.

2. J. W. L. Beament (ed.), *Models and Analogues in Biology*, Cambridge University Press 1960; Hans Freudenthal (ed.), *The Concept and the Role of the Model in Mathematics and Natural and Social Sciences*, Gordon & Breach 1961.

3. M. R. Cohen and E. Nagel, *An Introduction to Logic and Scientific Method*, Harcourt, Brace & Co. 1934, chap. 7. See also P. Suppes' essay in Freudenthal, op. cit.

4. E. Farber, 'Chemical Discoveries by Means of Analogies', *Isis*, vol. 41, 1950, p. 20; M. B. Hesse, 'Models in Physics', *British Journal for the Philosophy of Science*, vol. 4, 1953, p. 198; E. H. Hutten, 'The Role of Models in Physics', ibid., vol. 4, 1953, p. 284.

5. Mary B. Hesse, *Models and Analogies in Science*, Sheed & Ward 1963, chap. 1.

6. Mary B. Hesse, 'Models and Analogy in Science', in P. Edwards (ed.), *Encyclopedia of Philosophy*, vol. 5, p. 356.

7. Jacques Hadamard, *Essay on the Psychology of Invention in the Mathematical Field*, Princeton University Press 1964; Brewster Ghiselin (ed.), *The Creative Process*, University of California Press 1952.

8. Jerome B. Wiesner, 'Education for Creativity in the Sciences', *Daedalus*, vol. 94, 1965, p. 527; Arthur Koestler, *The Act of Creation*, Hutchinson's University Library and Macmillan 1964, chaps. 8, 10.

9. N. R. Campbell, *Physics, the Elements*, Cambridge University Press 1920 (paperback edition entitled *Foundations of Science*), chap. 4.

10. William Thomson (Lord Kelvin), *Baltimore Lectures*, John Hopkins University 1904, p. 187.

11. Examples of the positivist position are cited in Ian G. Barbour, *Issues in Science and Religion*, SCM Press and Prentice Hall 1966, pp. 163f.

12. Stephen Toulmin, *The Philosophy of Science*, Hutchinson's University Library 1953.

13. Cited in Black, *Models and Metaphors*, p. 236.

14. Richard Braithwaite, *Scientific Explanation*, Cambridge University Press 1953, p. 92. See also Ernest Nagel, *The Structure of Science*, Routledge & Kegan Paul and Harcourt, Brace & World 1961, pp. 107–117; Peter Caws, *The Philosophy of Science*, D. Van Nostrand 1965, chap. 19.

15. See Barbour, *Issues in Sciences and Religion*, pp. 172–174.

16. Marshall Spector, 'Models and Theories', *British Journal for the Philosophy of Science*, vol. 16, 1965, p. 135.

17. Leonard Nash, *The Nature of Natural Science*, Little, Brown and Co. 1963, p. 251. Here, as throughout the present volume, all italics shown within quotations are in the original text.

18. Braithwaite, op. cit., chap. 4.

19. Hesse, *Models and Analogies in Science*, pp. 34–37.

20. Peter Achinstein, 'Models, Analogies and Theories', *Philosophy of Science*, vol. 31, 1964, p. 328; also 'Theoretical Models', *British Journal for the Philosophy of Science*, vol. 16, 1965, p. 102.

21. Spector, loc. cit., pp. 121ff.; J. W. Swanson, 'On Models', *British Journal for the Philosophy of Science*, vol. 17, 1967, p. 297.

22. Nash, op. cit., pp. 230–253.

23. C. G. Hempel and P. Oppenheim, 'The Logic of Explanation', in H. Feigl and M. Brodbeck, (eds), *Readings in the Philosophy of Science*, Appleton-Century-Crofts 1953.

24. Israel Scheffler, *The Anatomy of Inquiry*, Alfred A. Knopf 1963, pp. 43ff.; Michael Scriven, 'Explanation and Prediction in Evolutionary Theory', *Science*, vol. 130, 1959, p. 477; see also the essays in Part II of B. Baumrin (ed.), *Philosophy of Science: The Delaware Seminar*, Interscience Publishers 1963, vol. I.

25. Stephen Toulmin, *Foresight and Understanding*, Hutchinson's University Library and Indiana University Press 1961.

26. Nagel, op. cit., p. 114.

27. Black, *Models and Metaphors*, p. 237.

28. Mary B. Hesse, 'The Explanatory Function of Metaphor', in Y. Bar-Hillel (ed.), *Logic, Methodology and Philosophy of Science* Amsterdam: North Holland Publishing Co. 1965; reprinted in the US edition only of *Models and Analogies in Science*, University of Notre Dame Press 1966, pp. 164–165.

29. Donald Schon, *The Displacement of Concepts*, Tavistock Publications 1963 (paperback edition entitled *Invention and the Evolution of Ideas*). See also C. M. Turbayne, *The Myth of Metaphor*, Yale University Press 1962.

30. R. Harré, *Theories and Things*, Sheed & Ward 1961, p. 41.

31. See notes 27 and 28 above.

32. *The Scientific Papers of James Clerk Maxwell*, Cambridge University Press 1890, vol. I, p. 160.

33. Max Born, *Philosophical Quarterly*, vol. 3, 1953, p. 140.

Chapter 4   MODELS IN RELIGION

1. Ludwig Wittgenstein, *Philosophical Investigations*, Basil Blackwell 1953, p. 194e.

2. John Wisdom, 'Gods', *Proceedings of the Aristotelian Society*, vol. 45, 1944, p. 187; reprinted in Antony Flew (ed.), *Logic and Language*, vol. I, Basil Blackwell 1951.

3. John Wisdom, *Paradox and Discovery*, Basil Blackwell 1965, p. 54.

4. John Hick, *Faith and Knowledge*, 2nd ed. Macmillan 1967, pp. 142f.

5. Ibid., p. 122; see also John Hick, 'Religious Faith as Experiencing-As', in G. N. A. Vesey (ed.), *Talk of God*, Macmillan 1969.

6. Rudolf Otto, *The Idea of the Holy* trans. J. W. Harvey, Oxford University

Press 1923; see also Langdon Gilkey, *Naming the Whirlwind*, Bobbs Merrill Co. 1969; H. D. Lewis, *Our Experience of God*, Allen & Unwin 1959.

7. Peter Berger, *A Rumor of Angels*, Doubleday and Co. 1969, chap. 3; Donald Evans, 'Differences between Scientific and Religious Assertions', in Ian G. Barbour (ed.), *Science and Religion: New Perspectives on the Dialogue*, Harper & Row 1968.

8. See Paul Tillich, *The Shaking of the Foundations*, Charles Scribner's Sons 1948, pp. 162ff.

9. Martin Buber, *I and Thou* trans. R. G. Smith, T. & T. Clark 1937; and *Between Man and Man*, Macmillan 1947.

10. H. Richard Niebuhr, *The Meaning of Revelation*, Macmillan 1941, chap. 3.

11. See John Cobb, *A Christian Natural Theology*, Westminster Press 1965, for a recent example.

12. Richard Braithwaite, *An Empiricist's View of the Nature of Religious Belief*, Cambridge University Press 1955, reprinted in John Hick (ed.), *The Existence of God*, Macmillan 1964, p. 239.

13. Ibid., pp. 246–247.

14. Ibid., p. 249.

15. T. R. Miles, *Religion and the Scientific Outlook*, Allen & Unwin 1959, p. 74.

16. Ibid., p. 178.

17. Donald Evans, *The Logic of Self-Involvement*, SCM Press 1963, chap. 3.

18. Ibid., pp. 227, 251.

19. Ian Ramsey, *Models and Mystery*, Oxford University Press 1964, p. 17.

20. See Ian Ramsey, *Christian Discourse*, Oxford University Press 1965, pp. 25, 60, 82.

21. Ramsey, *Models and Mystery*, p. 20.

22. Ibid., pp. 58, 61.

23. Ian Ramsey, *Religious Language*, SCM Press 1957, chap. 2.

24. Ibid., p. 79.

25. See William Austin, 'Models, Mystery, and Paradox in Ian Ramsey', *Journal for the Scientific Study of Religion*, vol. 7, 1968, p. 41.

26. Ramsey, *Religious Language*, chap. 1.

27. Dorothy Emmet, *The Nature of Metaphysical Thinking*, Macmillan 1949, p. 215.

28. Stephen Pepper, *World Hypotheses*, University of California Press 1942.

29. Frederick Ferré, 'Mapping the Logic of Models in Science and Theology', *The Christian Scholar*, vol. 46, 1963, p. 31.

30. Frederick Ferré, *Basic Modern Philosophy of Religion*, Charles Scribner's Sons 1967, p. 381.

31. Frederick Ferré, 'Metaphors, Models and Religion', *Soundings*, vol. 51, 1968, pp. 341–342.

32. C. H. Whiteley, 'The Cognitive Factor in Religious Experience', *Aristotelian Society Supplementary Volume 29*, 1955, p. 85.

Chapter 5 COMPLEMENTARY MODELS

1. See, for example, Philipp Frank, *Philosophy of Science*, Bailey Bros & Swinfen and Prentice Hall 1957, chap. 9. A very readable account is given in Richard Feynman, *The Character of Physical Law*, MIT Press 1967.

2. Ernest Nagel, *The Structure of Science*, pp. 300, 302.

3. Mary B. Hesse, *Forces and Fields*, Thomas Nelson and Sons 1961, p. 23. See also *Models and Analogies in Science*, pp. 57ff.

4. Ernest H. Hutten, *The Language of Modern Physics*, Allen & Unwin and Macmillan 1956, p. 164.

5. Mary Hesse in D. Bohm et al., *Quanta and Reality*, World Publishing Co. 1964, p. 57.

6. Niels Bohr, *Atomic Theory and the Description of Nature*, Cambridge University Press 1934, p. 96.

7. Niels Bohr, *Atomic Physics and Human Knowledge*, Chapman & Hall and John Wiley & Sons 1958, pp. 39ff.

8. Ibid., pp. 92ff. See also Gerald Holton, 'The Roots of Complementarity', *Daedalus*, vol. 99, 1970, p. 1015; J. Robert Oppenheimer, *Science and the Common Understanding*, Oxford University Press and Simon and Schuster 1954, chaps. 4–6.

9. C. A. Coulson, *Science and Christian Belief*, Oxford University Press and University of North Carolina Press 1955, chap. 3.

10. D. M. MacKay, 'Complementarity', *Aristotelian Society Supplementary Volume 32*, 1958, p. 105.

11. P. K. Feyerabend, 'Problems of Microphysics', in R. G. Colodny (ed.), *Frontiers of Science and Philosophy*, Allen & Unwin and University of Pittsburgh Press 1962.

12. Peter Alexander, 'Complementary Descriptions', *Mind*, vol. 65, 1956, p. 145.

13. Ninian Smart, *Reasons and Faiths*, Routledge & Kegan Paul 1958; *World Religions: A Dialogue*, Penguin Books 1969; *The Concept of Worship*, Macmillan 1972; 'Revelation, Reason and Religions' in Ian Ramsey (ed.), *Prospect for Metaphysics*, Allen & Unwin 1961.

14. Winston King, *Introduction to Religion: A Phenomenological Approach*, Harper & Row 1968, p. 165.

15. W. T. Stace, *Mysticism and Philosophy*, Lippincott 1960; see also William James, *Varieties of Religious Experience*, Collier-Macmillan and Random House n.d.

16. G. van der Leeuw, *Religion in Essence and Manifestation*, p. 501.

17. Versions from Omar Khayyam, Mahmud, and the Upanishads are quoted in ibid, p. 498.

18. See especially *Reasons and Faiths*.

19. M. Conrad Hyers, 'Prophet and Mystic: Toward a Phenomenological Foundation for a World Ecumenicity', *Cross Currents*, Fall 1970, p. 435.

20. King, *Introduction to Religion*, pp. 20–21.

21. Ibid., p. 152.

22. S. Radhakrishnan, *Recovery of Faith*, Allen & Unwin 1956, p. 155.

23. Eckhart, *Mystische Schriften*, p. 122, quoted in Evelyn Underhill, *Mysticism*, Methuen & Co. 1911, p. 418.

24. William Austin, 'Waves, Particles and Paradoxes', *Rice University Studies*, vol. 53, 1967, pp. 93ff.

25. Paul Tillich, *The Courage to Be*, Yale University Press 1952, chap. 6.

26. Paul Tillich, *Biblical Religion and the Search for Ultimate Reality*, University of Chicago Press 1955.

27. Paul Tillich, *Systematic Theology*, vol. II, University of Chicago Press 1957, pp. 5–10.

28. Paul Tillich, *Systematic Theology*, vol. I, University of Chicago Press 1951, p. 245.

29. *Biblical Religion and the Search for Ultimate Reality*, pp. 83–84.

30. Paul Tillich, *Dynamics of Faith*, Harper & Row 1957, chap. 3; also 'The Meaning and Justification of Religious Symbols', in Sidney Hook (ed.), *Religious Experience and Truth*, New York University Press 1961.

31. *Systematic Theology*, vol. II, pp. 97–180.

32. Paul Tillich, *The Shaking of the Foundations* and *The New Being*, Charles Scribner's Sons 1955.

33. *Systematic Theology*, vol. I, Part II.

34. Paul Tillich, 'Two Types of Philosophy of Religion', in *Theology of Culture*, Oxford University Press 1964.

Chapter 6 PARADIGMS IN SCIENCE

1. Richard Braithwaite, *Scientific Explanation*; Carl G. Hempel, *Aspects of Scientific Explanation*, The Free Press 1965; Karl R. Popper, *The Logic of Scientific Discovery*, Hutchinson's University Library 1956. Popper calls his view critical rationalism rather than empiricism because observation-sentences are used to falsify rather than to verify theories. In Ernest Nagel, *The Structure of Science*, the distinction between theory and observation is less absolute than for these other authors.

2. Toulmin, *Foresight and Understanding*; N. R. Hanson, *Patterns of Discovery*, Cambridge University Press 1958; Michael Polanyi, *Personal Knowledge*, University of Chicago Press 1958. References on Feyerabend and Kuhn are given below.

3. P. K. Feyerabend, 'Explanation, Reduction and Empiricism', in H. Feigl and G. Maxwell (eds.), *Minnesota Studies in the Philosophy of Science*, vol. 3, University of Minnesota Press 1962; also 'Problems of Empiricism', in R. Colodny (ed.), *Beyond the Edge of Certainty*, Prentice-Hall 1965.

4. P. K. Feyerabend, 'Problems of Empiricism, Part 2', in R. Colodny (ed.),

The Nature and Function of Scientific Theory, University of Pittsburgh Press 1971.

5. Israel Scheffler, *Science and Subjectivity*, The Bobbs-Merrill Co. 1967, p. 44.

6. Ibid., p. 119.

7. Mary Hesse, 'Theory and Observation: Is There an Independent Observation Language?', in Colodny (ed.), *The Nature and Function of Scientific Theory*.

8. Popper, *The Logic of Scientific Discovery*. Also *Conjectures and Refutations*, Routledge & Kegan Paul 1963.

9. See Irving M. Copi, 'Crucial Experiments', in E. H. Madden (ed.), *The Structure of Science*, Houghton Mifflin Co. 1960.

10. W. V. Quine, *From a Logical Point of View*, Harvard University Press 1953, p. 43.

11. Imre Lakatos, 'Falsification and the Methodology of Scientific Research Programmes', in I. Lakatos and A. Musgrave, *Criticism and the Growth of Knowledge*, Cambridge University Press 1970, p. 130. This volume is cited as *CGK* in subsequent footnotes.

12. *CGK*, p. 128.

13. *CGK*, pp. 159ff.; also Lakatos, 'History of Science and Its Rational Reconstructions', in R. Buck and R. Cohen (eds.), *Boston Studies in the Philosophy of Science*, vol. 8, D. Reidel Publishing Co. 1971, p. 100.

14. See R. G. Swinburne, 'The Falsifiability of Scientific Theories', *Mind*, July 1964, p. 434; W. Whewell, *History of the Inductive Sciences*, rev. ed. 1847, vol. II, p. 220. Other examples are given in Polanyi, op. cit., pp. 148–158.

15. *CGK*, p. 133.

16. Eugene Lashchyk, *Scientific Revolutions*, Ph.D. dissertation, University of Pennsylvania 1969.

17. Thomas S. Kuhn, *The Structure of Scientific Revolutions*, University of Chicago Press 1962, p. 10.

18. Ibid., p. 24.

19. Ibid., pp. 147, 149.

20. Ibid., chap. 10.

21. Ibid., p. 6.

22. Ibid., chap. 12.

23. Margaret Masterman, 'The Nature of a Paradigm'; K. R. Popper, 'Normal Science and its Dangers'; P. K. Feyerabend, 'Consolations for the Specialist'; all in *CGK*.

24. S. E. Toulmin, 'Does the Distinction between Normal and Revolutionary Science Hold Water?', in *CGK*.

25. Dudley Shapere, 'Meaning and Scientific Change', in R. Colodny (ed.), *Mind and Cosmos*, University of Pittsburgh Press 1966. See also Scheffler, op. cit., chap. 4.

26. *CGK*, pp. 93, 178.

27. J. W. N. Watkins, 'Against "Normal Science"', in *CGK*, p. 33.

28. *CGK*, pp. 56, 57.

29. Thomas Kuhn, *The Structure of Scientific Revolutions*, 2nd ed. University of Chicago Press 1970, pp.187–191. See also his 'Second Thoughts on Paradigms', in Frederick Suppe (ed.), *The Structure of Scientific Theories*, University of Illinois Press 1973.

30. *Structure of Scientific Revolutions*, 2nd ed., p.184.

31. Ibid., p.181. Also Kuhn, 'Reflections on my Critics', in *CGK*, p.249.

32. *Structure of Scientific Revolutions*, 2nd ed., p.201.

33. Ibid., p.185.

34. Ibid., pp.199–200.

35. Ibid., pp.205–206. See also Kuhn, 'Notes on Lakatos', in *Boston Studies in Philosophy of Science*, vol. 8, pp.144ff.

36. Dudley Shapere, 'The Paradigm Concept', *Science*, vol. 172, 1971, pp. 708–709.

37. See William Austin, 'Paradigms, Rationality and Partial Communication', *Journal of General Philosophy of Science* (to appear in 1973).

38. F. Schillp (ed.), *Albert Einstein: Philosopher-Scientist*, Library of Living Philosophers 1949, p.53.

39. Mary Hesse, 'Models of Theory Change', in Proceedings of the IVth International Congress of Logic, Methodology and Philosophy of Science, Bucharest, 1971 (to be published).

Chapter 7 PARADIGMS IN RELIGION

1. See, for example, John Dewey, *Experience and Nature*, Open Court Publishing Co. 1929; John E. Smith, *Experience and God*, Oxford University Press 1968. The theory of experience outlined here is indebted to American pragmatism, *Gestalt* psychology, and process philosophy.

2. See note 6 in chap.4 above.

3. Ninian Smart, 'Interpretation and Mystical Experience', *Religious Studies*, vol. 1, 1965, p.75.

4. Ronald Hepburn, *Christianity and Paradox*, C. A. Watts Co. and Humanities Press 1958; also his 'Religious Experience' in P. Edwards (ed.), *Encyclopedia of Philosophy*, vol.7. See also C. B. Martin, *Religious Belief*, Oxford University Press and Cornell University Press 1959; William Hamilton, 'Questions and Answers on the Radical Theology', in J. L. Ice and J. J. Carey (eds.), *The Death of God Debate*, Westminster Press 1967.

5. Peter Munz, *Problems of Religious Knowledge*, SCM Press 1959; J. H. Randall, *The Role of Knowledge in Western Religion*, Beacon Press 1958.

6. Anders Jeffner, *The Study of Religious Language*, SCM Press 1972, pp.45, 116, 125.

7. John Hick, *Faith and Knowledge*, 2nd ed. chap.6.

8. See John E. Smith, op. cit., pp.52, 84.

9. Antony Flew, 'Theology and Falsification', in A. Flew and A. Mac-

Intyre (eds.), *New Essays in Philosophical Theology*, SCM Press 1955, pp.98–99.

10. Flew's position is defended by e.g. Kai Nielsen, 'On Fixing the Reference Range of "God"', *Religious Studies*, vol.2, 1966, p.1 and *Contemporary Critiques of Religion*, Macmillan 1971. See also J. Kellenberger, 'The Falsification Challenge', *Religious Studies*, vol.5, 1969, p.69; reply by Flew, op. cit., p.77, and Kellenberger's rebuttal, op. cit., p.243.

11. D. Z. Phillips, *Faith and Philosophical Enquiry*, Routledge & Kegan Paul 1970, chaps 1–5.

12. See F. Michael McLain, 'Analysis, Metaphysics, and Belief', *Religious Studies*, vol.5, 1969, p.29.

13. Basil Mitchell, 'Theology and Falsification', in Flew and MacIntyre (eds.), *New Essays*.

14. Ibid., p.105.

15. Ian Crombie, 'Theology and Falsification', in Flew and MacIntyre, op. cit.; John Hick, *Faith and Knowledge*.

16. Howard Burkle, 'Counting Against and Counting Decisively Against', *Journal of Religion*, vol.44, 1964, p.227; see also Paul Clifford, 'The Factual Reference of Theological Assertions', *Religious Studies*, vol.3, 1967, p.339.

17. John F. Miller III, 'Science and Religion: Their Logical Similarity', *Religious Studies*, vol.5, 1969, p.64.

18. John King-Farlow and William N. Christensen, 'Faith – and Faith in Hypotheses', *Religious Studies*, vol.7, 1971, p.113.

19. Norman Siefferman, 'Science and Religion: A Reply to John F. Miller', *Religious Studies*, vol.6, 1970, p.281.

20. Barbour, *Issues in Science and Religion*, pp.229–236.

21. See William Austin, 'Religious Commitment and the Logical Status of Doctrines', *Religious Studies*, vol.9, 1973, p.39.

22. William James, *The Will to Believe*, Longmans, Green & Co. 1921; F. R. Tennant, *Philosophical Theology*, Cambridge University Press 1930.

23. H. H. Price, 'Belief "In" and Belief "That"', *Religious Studies*, vol.1, 1965, p.1.

24. This paragraph and the following one are developed more fully in *Issues in Science and Religion*, pp.226ff.

25. See R. N. Smart, 'Myth and Transcendence', *The Monist*, vol.50, 1966, p.475.

26. Lawrence C. Becker, 'A Note on Religious Experience Arguments', *Religious Studies*, vol.7, 1971, p.63.

27. Ian Ramsey makes this point frequently, e.g. *Religious Language*, chap.1. See Donald Evans, 'Ian Ramsey on Talk about God', *Religious Studies*, vol.7, 1971, pp.125, 213.

28. Ian Ramsey, *Religious Language*, pp.59f.; also *Religion and Science*, SPCK 1966, pp.73f. For other views of the relation between religion and metaphysics, see Ian Ramsey (ed.), *Prospect for Metaphysics*; Frank Dilley,

Metaphysics and Religious Language, Columbia University Press 1964; James Richmond, *Theology and Metaphysics*, SCM Press 1970.

29. E. D. Klemke, 'Are Religious Statements Meaningful?', *Journal of Religion*, vol.40, 1960, p.27; R. G. Collingwood, *An Essay on Metaphysics*, Oxford University Press 1940.

Chapter 8 THE CHRISTIAN PARADIGM

1. Paul Tillich, *The Shaking of the Foundations*, pp.162ff.; also *Systematic Theology*, vol. II.
2. William Austin, 'Waves, Particles and Paradoxes', *Rice University Studies*, vol.53, 1967, pp.85ff.
3. Ibid., p.90.
4. John McIntyre, *The Shape of Christology*, SCM Press and Westminster Press 1966.
5. Ibid., p.173.
6. Ibid., pp.73ff.
7. Ibid., pp.173, 175.
8. Ibid., pp.79–81.
9. See Ewart Cousins, 'Models and the Future of Theology', *Continuum*, vol.7, 1969, p.84.
10. Some of these atonement models are discussed in Ramsey, *Christian Discourse*, chap.2.
11. See Alan R. White (ed.), *The Philosophy of Action*, Oxford University Press 1968; Norman Care and Charles Landesman, *Readings in the Theory of Action*, Indiana University Press 1968.
12. Gordon Kaufman, 'On the Meaning of "Act of God"', *Harvard Theological Review*, vol.61, 1968, p.175.
13. John J. Compton, 'Science and God's Action in Nature', in Ian G. Barbour (ed.), *Earth Might Be Fair; Reflections on Ethics, Religion and Ecology*, Prentice-Hall 1972, p.39.
14. Kai Nielsen, *Contemporary of Religion*, chap. 6; cf. Paul Edwards, 'Difficulties in the Idea of God', and reply by Donald Evans, in E. H. Madden, R. Handy and M. Farber (eds.), *The Idea of God*, Charles Thomas 1968.
15. Robert King, 'The Conceivability of God', *Religious Studies*, vol. 9, 1973, p.39; see also his *The Meaning of God*, Fortress Press 1973.
16. Compton, op. cit., pp.42, 47.
17. I have discussed process thought at greater length in *Issues in Science and Religion*, chap.13, and *Science and Secularity*, pp.46–57.
18. Alfred North Whitehead, *Process and Reality*, Allen & Unwin and Macmillan 1929; Ivor Leclerc, *Whitehead's Metaphysics*, Macmillan 1958; William Christian, *An Interpretation of Whitehead's Metaphysics*, Yale University Press 1959.

19. Whitehead, *Process and Reality*, p. 532.

20. Charles Hartshorne, *The Divine Relativity*, Yale University Press 1948, p. 90.

21. Charles Hartshorne, *Reality as Social Process*, The Free Press 1953, p. 142; also *The Logic of Perfection*, Open Court Publishing Co. 1962, chap. 7 and *Man's Vision of God*, Willett, Clark & Co. 1941, chap. 5.

22. Cobb, *A Christian Natural Theology*, p. 189.

23. For example, John B. Cobb, *God and the World*, Westminster Press 1969; Eugene Peters, *The Creative Advance*, Bethany Press 1966; Peter Hamilton, *The Living God and the Modern World*, Hodder & Stoughton and Pilgrim Press 1967; Norman Pittenger, *Alfred North Whitehead*, John Knox Press 1969.

24. J. N. Findlay, 'Can God's Existence Be Disproved?' in Flew and MacIntyre (eds.), *New Essays*.

25. H. P. Owen, *Concepts of Deity*, Macmillan 1971, p. 57.

26. Peter Appleby, 'On Religious Attitudes', *Religious Studies*, vol. 6, 1970, p. 359.

27. Pierre Teilhard de Chardin, *The Future of Man* trans. N. Denny, Collins and Harper & Row 1964, p. 90.

28. See Ian G. Barbour, 'Attitudes toward Nature and Technology', in Barbour (ed.), *Earth Might Be Fair*; also John B. Cobb, *Is It Too Late?* Bruce Publishing Co. 1972.

Chapter 9 CONCLUSIONS

1. Robert N. Bellah, 'Religion in the University: Changing Consciousness, Changing Structures', in Claude Welch (ed.), *Religion in the Undergraduate Curriculum*, Association of American Colleges, 1972, p. 14.

2. Robert N. Bellah, 'Christianity and Symbolic Realism', *Journal for the Scientific Study of Religion*, vol. 9, 1970, p. 93.

3. G. van der Leeuw, *Religion in Essence and Manifestation*; Mircea Eliade, *The Sacred and the Profane*; Joseph Bettis (ed.), *Phenomenology of Religion*, Harper & Row 1969.

4. See, for example, Frederick J. Streng, *Understanding Religious Man*, Dickenson 1969; Walter Capps (ed.), *Ways of Understanding Religion*, Macmillan 1972.

5. Owen C. Thomas (ed.), *Attitudes Toward Other Religions*, Harper & Row 1969.

6. M. A. C. Warren, Introduction to John V. Taylor, *The Primal Vision: Christian Presence Amid African Religion*, SCM Press 1963, p. 7.

7. I have elaborated on this theme in the concluding essay in Barbour (ed.), *Earth Might Be Fair*.

8. See, for example, Martin Marty and Dean Peerman (eds.), *New Theology No. 8*, Macmillan 1971.

INDEX OF NAMES